WORKING
IN
AMERICA

SPECTATOR OR GLADIATOR…
YOU DECIDE

CHOSEN VESSELS ™
PUBLISHING & ENTERTAINMENT

MICHAEL A. MASON

CHOSEN VESSELS ™

Publishing & Entertainment

Published by Chosen Vessels Publishing and Entertainment (USA) Inc.

Jacksonville, Florida 32210 U.S.A.

Second Printing

Copyright © 2022 Michael A. Mason All rights reserved

Chosen Vessels Publishing & Entertainment, Inc.

REGISTERED TRADEMARK

ISBN – 978-0-578-35498-9

Printed in the United States of America

Book Cover by: Oliviaprodesign

Editor: Merdis (Penny) Dickerson

PUBLISHER'S NOTE

Working in America
Spectator or Gladiator…You Decide

Dedication

This book is dedicated first to three very important people in my life. My sons Matthew and Benjamin and their wonderful mother Susan. They were my inspiration as so much of my professional life would not have been possible save for their willingness to relocate and acclimate to different cities and schools many times across the expanse of my professional life. Their adaptability and Susan's drive to make every house we purchased a warm, cozy home is what gave me the latitude to do the work I was always so grateful to be able to do. I owe my undying gratitude to Susan, Matthew and Benjamin.

Secondly, I dedicate this book to the wonderful village that raised me on the Southside of Chicago. This village included my family, neighbors (some of whom readers of this book will meet), teachers, coaches and bosses I had while working as a teenager and young man. There is not room on this page nor in this book to adequately express my love and appreciation to all of the people to whom I am referring to here. Sadly, many of them have now passed on, but through me and many others they touched, taught and nurtured, their legacies live on.

So to my grandparents Jack, Bert, Bill and Thelma, my father Howard, my brothers Howard and James and sisters Lynn and Anita, my step-mother Marlene, countless neighbors, bosses and coaches to include Audrey and Bob Wright, Rodney Wright, Mr. Fleming, Mrs. Williamson (and her entire family), Willie Bradley, Mr. Curtin, Mr. Powell and many, many others… thank you from the very depth of my heart. Each of you owns a piece of this book. I love you all.

Finally, a special thank you to my dear friend Bob White, who was the first person to see the rough manuscript and his help editing the first manuscript was invaluable. His willingness to do a very detailed reading of the rough draft is greatly appreciated. Thank you all.

Foreword

Why this book, why this time? I have had a lot of people suggest to me that I should write a book about thriving in America's professional arena. I have genuinely enjoyed my entire professional life and every job I have ever held. People have asked me about the secret of my success. I feel that my success has less to do with the professional roles I have had than the attitude I have brought to each. The intent of this book is categorically not to *define success* as I believe that definition must be customized by each one of us.

Browsing the aisles of bookstores remains a favorite pastime of mine, and I am frequently drawn to titles that illuminate the navigation of one's professional life. Intrigued, I wondered how I could endeavor to write on the subject but convey something different regarding the path to success. My personal collection contains an array of books on the subject, and in my opinion, many lack a degree of specificity and insight as to how the authors traversed their own white-water rapids.

Some of the books I have read have been written by academics rather than practitioners and that, too, has been a point weakening my embrace of much of the advice I have read. This is not a criticism of academics. An academic could read hot washes (operational reviews) from SWAT operations executed around the country and likely offer sound advice to SWAT operators on how to execute dynamic arrests more effectively. However, as a former SWAT operator, I would undoubtedly come to a piece of their offering that informed me immediately that they had never actually engaged in an real SWAT operation. As a student and practitioner of all contained in this book and being very happy with the success I have enjoyed in three distinctly different environments, i.e., U.S. military, U.S. civilian government and the private sector, I hope this will reduce hip-pocket responses such as "That could never happen in the *real world*," or "*If I ever tried that I'd be out of a job."* Every story contained in this book is from the very real professional environments in which I have worked.

I spent five years as an officer in the United States Marine Corps rising to the rank of captain, 23 years with the Federal Bureau of Investigation where I retired as an Executive Assistant Director (4th on the FBI's food chain at that time), and 13 years in the private sector where I retired as a Senior Vice-President and Chief Security Officer for a Fortune 20 company. I loved just about every day of my professional life despite having faced many challenges along the way. I am grateful for the outstanding mentors I have been so fortunate to have throughout the entirety of my professional life. Absent the presence of excellent mentors at critical junctures along my academic and professional journey, I suspect what you are preparing to read would not have been possible. I am grateful to more people than I can easily name who served as guideposts for me as I pursued my professional goals. I hope what sets this book apart from many others are the stories I have shared which reflect the manner in which I navigated the white-water rapids of my own professional journey. I am sharing these stories with the intention of showing practical, real-life examples of challenging situations I have faced in my professional life and the solutions I used to effectively address them.

My intention in sharing the stories contained herein is to encourage movement from seats occupied by spectators and into the arena as *gladiators*. Stop looking for the perfect environment where racism, sexism, homophobia, and the other afflictions of society no longer exist. Society must obviously continue to work hard to eliminate such negative influences, but what about you? How do you navigate your own professional white-water rapids… *right now*? The subtitle, "Spectator or Gladiator…You Decide" describes one of two roles I feel we all get to choose, whether at work, on a team, or in any of life's pursuits. We get to decide every day of the week the role we will play in shaping the world in which we exist. Is it possible for one person change the dynamics within their workplace single-handedly? Not likely, but we can all contribute in a variety of positive ways, even if that is to influence one person at a time. It is a challenge to stop thinking with the herd and stand on your own to address a situation you feel must be corrected, whether that situation impacts you directly or someone close to you. This is a call to stop seeking standard, bandwagon safe harbors every time a situation begs for the intervention of someone…especially when that *someone* can and often should be **_you_**

Chapter One

Growing Up Gladiator

"Every story contained in this book stems from the actual, professional work environments in which I have engaged."

-Michael A. Mason

My unapologetic intent in drafting this book is to encourage those who find themselves wanting more out of their careers than they are currently receiving to step back and examine the reasons why they have not self-actualized. I have met many people who are perfectly content with their job, position, salary, commute and all the other components that make up one's working world. There is nothing wrong with that at all. Those employees are the oil that keeps the machine running. They are integral to the success of any business. However, this book was not written for those folks.

I have met and mentored literally hundreds of people who desire much more than their current lot in life. They believe they have the ability to manage and lead and they possess a strong desire to do so. However, they often find themselves constrained by the relatively low level of their current position. They have embraced faulty notions, such as wanting to maintain a low profile for fear of looking too ambitious. They fail to speak up in meetings, fearing their voice will be quashed by those of a higher rank. They believe self-promotion is synonymous with undermining their fellow employees. Finally, they often feel as though they are ready to begin the journey into management, but ironically, they lack the confidence to develop a plan and execute it. It is for these people this book was written. I was motivated to write this book after years of mentoring employees who were utterly dissatisfied with their current position but had little to offer when questioned regarding what steps they had taken to change the course of their professional life.

The subtitle of this book— "Spectator or Gladiator...You Decide"— is its core theme. It is a narrative based on my real-life experiences from the age of ten until I retired from the corporate world as a senior executive.

My approach is designed to help you find the courage to step up and act when the moment calls for you to do so. It is also a challenge to stop thinking with the herd and stand on your own to address a situation you feel needs to be addressed.

Why did I choose the example of ancient gladiators and spectators as a backdrop to the professional behaviors of America's current workforce? The parallels are keen, and they consistently conjure relatable images. Gladiators had to fight for their lives. They could not simply wish for a better life or wake up and hope they would fight well today. They had to prepare knowing that failure could quite literally result in the loss of their life. Each one had to face each day focused on being better than their next opponent. They had to fight for themselves as no one else possibly could. Gladiators undoubtedly had to overcome their own internal fears and the fear that the next opponent could be a better fighter.

The solutions to become a successful gladiator seem strikingly like achieving success today. The superior gladiators trained hard to learn their craft. In overcoming their opponents, they had to enter the arena completely confident of their skills and abilities.

While they long to advance, too many employees unknowingly develop a visual acuity that only allows them to see barriers to achievement rather than opportunities for success. Instead of nurturing their own passion to succeed, they become resentful spectators of those who advance and despondent at their own failure to do so. What was envisioned as an exciting career

2

offering potential for advancement and an opportunity for a level of financial independence has instead become a mere job. What was described as a ladder to success by human resources has failed to materialize as anticipated. Such employees begin to see a divided workforce and develop an *us against them* attitude. In the worst-case scenario, these employees cease to pursue advancement and instead actively seek to avoid the very kind of work challenges that could propel them to the next level.

The players become spiteful spectators, harboring resentful attitudes that ironically only hamper any hopes of upward advancement. Their entire work experience becomes cyclic: a vibrant introduction to their new work environment followed by a slow erosion of attitude and focus when the career they envisioned appears to have stalled.

Far too often, I have heard that one's movement within a company has been precluded because of race, sex, religion, sexual orientation, or age.

While our history gives credence to such causes impacting the trajectory of one's career, no one desirous of leadership positions should cruise into those safe harbors and simply stop. Why do I refer to such causes as *safe harbors*? When we stop pursuing our goals because of these things, we relieve ourselves of any additional responsibility to continue engaging. We relieve ourselves of any additional self-reflection because we embrace the idea that we were already as competitive as possible and, as a result, our failure to achieve the desired outcome *must* be attributable to something we cannot control. We allow ourselves to become spectators.

I have loved just about every day of my professional life, despite having faced challenges along the way, as both student and practitioner. Every story contained in this book stems from the actual professional work environments in which I have engaged. I am very proud of the success I have enjoyed in three distinctly different environments. Following college graduation from Illinois Wesleyan University in Bloomington, Illinois, I was commissioned into the United States Marine Corp as a second lieutenant, followed by 23 years in the Federal Bureau of Investigation (FBI), and finally, 13 years with Verizon as a senior vice-president Chief Security Officer. I grew up on the southside of Chicago raised by a single father who drove a truck for the Chicago Board of Education. My mother passed away within the first two years of my life, but my father did remarry. My step-mother, Marlene, was present in my life from the time I began kindergarten through the beginning of second grade. She left my father at that time. One evening she was packing items from the kitchen and I asked her what she was doing. She replied, "You will see in the morning." and the next day, she and my half-siblings, Ernest and Anita, were gone. My father and stepmother reconnected approximately eight years later. As a result of her absence during a critical period in my life, my father was ultimately the primary parent in my life and his influence on the man I was to become will become more apparent throughout this book. Although we lived a very modest lifestyle, you will soon learn I was rich in one thing, one thing far more important than material wealth: I was rich in the relationships I was so privileged to experience in the village of my childhood.

I was taught early of the pride of a hard day's work, and a strong desire to work as a young boy propelled me to ask for jobs at the age of nine or ten that most thought me too young to do well, and they were probably right.

Nonetheless, their faith in me always made me want to do the very best job I could do. Though I was often paid very little for hours of hard work, the lessons imparted by my neighbors were priceless. If you are intentional about your own professional development, seeking constant improvement in all that you do will be an essential component in your arsenal of weaponry. One quick, practical example to demonstrate my point:

Speaking before a roomful of people generally sits second or third on the list of things people fear the most. I, too, suffered from this fear. However, I also realized that to achieve my professional goals, I was going to have to become comfortable speaking before large audiences. As a result, in the early days of my FBI career I jumped at the chance to accept speaking engagements, regardless of the audience. I can vividly recall the first podium appearance I had as a young agent. I was asked to speak before a high school class consisting of approximately 35 students. How hard could that be? I thought about nine things I would speak about to the class. Why nine things? I figured the class was 45 minutes long and if I spoke on each topic for five minutes, I had sufficient material to cover the class period. That was the sum total of my preparation for my first speaking engagement.

When I arrived at the school, I was confident I was going to do well. After all, I already had five good years as a Marine Corps officer and now I was in the FBI. I was ready to knock them dead.

The reality is laughable *today* but taught me several invaluable lessons. First, I was finished with everything I could think to say in about seven minutes. When I realized I'd already run through my nine bullets, I looked at the clock and saw that only seven minutes had elapsed and I had an eager class of 35 students waiting for me to continue. I tapped danced a bit and eventually asked for questions, of which, thankfully, there were many. When I got back to my car, my dress shirt was completely drenched with sweat, to the extent that it had soaked through to my suit. I felt so embarrassed and ashamed because I knew in my heart, I had gone into that classroom utterly unprepared and believing that I could just *wing it*.

Lesson one*:* Preparation is your only ally. I'd accepted the assignment without so much as a five-minute conversation with the teacher of that class. I did not know what grade level I was addressing, the reason I was asked to come and speak, or the general interest of the students in the class. I knew nothing but wasn't smart enough to know what I didn't know.

Lesson two*:* Always know your audience and know what is expected of you. Is your presentation part of an ongoing discussion in the class? Is it to be career-focused, i.e., how does one prepare for a career in your world and are there particular areas

5

the teacher would like you to address? A presentation represents a relationship with your audience and if you care about developing your craft in this arena, you must be very intentional about the effort you put forth.

Although I have spoken to audiences comprised of hundreds of people—many times across my career—I have never stopped critically reviewing my performance after every single presentation I give. One of my very simple speaking goals is to leave without having committed a single error that will provide me with a cringe-worthy moment lasting well beyond the conclusion of my presentation. This is but one area of many by which I have been challenged over the past 40 years. I suspect many people who might have had a similar disaster in their first public speaking engagement never grew that capability any further because they decided in that moment they were never going to speak before another audience ever again. Not me. I knew what I had done wrong and was immediately ready to start working to get better. Please don't assume my next speaking engagement was Oscar worthy. It took a very long time to get comfortable speaking before large audiences, and as I mentioned above, it is a craft I continue to try and improve upon even today.

I completed my collegiate studies with a Bachelor of Science degree in accounting on May 18, 1980 and was commissioned as a second lieutenant in the U.S. Marine Corps on the same day. Marine Corps and FBI Special Agent training are both rigorous, allowing only small margins for error as one navigates the challenges each presented. Both of my chosen paths are also thematic to this book's title. In very different ways, both represented goals that I felt were going to stretch me. Both required the vanquishing of internal doubts.

A turning point for me occurred within my first four to five weeks of my freshman year in college during a conversation I had with my first Resident Assistant (RA). The RA was the individual responsible for keeping order on the floor, holding meet and greet events, and carrying out other responsibilities as directed by the residential staff. My first RA was a young man named Doug

Glasser, who was a smart, funny, and personable guy with a very calming presence.

One day he and I were having a conversation, the specifics of which have long faded away. However, during the conversation I remember saying, "Well, it's not like I am going to be great one day." Doug responded with words I will never forget. He said, "Why shouldn't you dare to be great?"

He was absolutely serious. Immediately after Doug and I finished our conversation, I took out my label maker and printed a label that read, "DARE TO BE GREAT." I had a General Electric alarm clock with a large face and placed that label on the front of that clock. Every day for the next five to six years, I woke to those words until the clock was no longer operable. What I took from Doug's words was not a message about setting a goal to be great as one might commonly consider greatness, but rather, dare to be the very best I could be. Dare to challenge my own conventional wisdom about myself.

Becoming a modern-day gladiator is not about vanquishing external adversaries, it is about conquering all the internal adversaries holding you back from reaching a peak point of self-actualization.

I never wanted to just get by—in the Marine Corps or in life. If you are not going to engage at full tilt, why engage at all? Why choose to watch others succeed and simply wish to be like them? I have always wanted to be in a greater arena, and the dream of joining the Marine Corps began for me sometime just before high school. However, the truth runs a bit deeper than my sitting around fostering a dream about one day becoming a Marine. My quest was birthed from an inward belief that I had never truly been tested by the rigors of life. In most of my athletic pursuits, I was average at best. I played (worked) hard, but was neither physically gifted nor naturally talented for sports such as baseball, basketball, and football, the last of which I only played with friends in the park and never with an organized team. I wasn't horrible at baseball or basketball, but I never once considered either something I was going to do to earn a living one day. I tried out for the cross-country team in high school but quit after the first day. I looked at stronger, faster, and bigger boys as just being naturally gifted. I never thought about getting better, rather I always thought I was not good enough. Working hard at the various jobs I held as a young teenager became my safe harbor. I *knew* how to work hard, but I needed more. I needed to know I could fight through my self-doubts and actually achieve something I initially deemed beyond my capabilities.

There are many existing myths about manhood, and American society advances the idea that boys and men are supposed to be tough. My life's storied beginning has a coming-of-age tale of its own that is comical upon reflection, but necessary when measuring how my attitudes about life evolved. When I was close to the age of 10 years old, I played in the park across the street from our Chicago home. The sandbox was a childhood favorite as I enjoyed building sandcastles. There was a little girl there as well, and at some point in our shared time in the sandbox, she accidentally, or purposefully, threw a small amount of sand on me. Well, I threw a little bit of sand back on her. It was not thrown directly in her face nor even on her body, just in her direction. Her brother, who was about 13 or 14 years old, witnessed this happen and promptly punched me in the head. A lump instantly appeared where I had been struck, and I decided my sandbox time was over for the day. I headed home in defeat and gently placed ice cubes in a hand towel and laid them on my newly acquired and painful wound.

My father sat attentively reading the daily paper and paid me no attention. I moaned just a bit to garner his attention, and after even more moaning than was warranted by the situation, my father lowered his paper and said, "Well boy, you'll either learn how to fight or learn how to avoid fights."

He then returned to reading the paper. That was it! I surmised that my father wanted nothing to do with coddling or even calling me over to look at my noggin injury. I also thought my father did not think I was very tough and that experiencing the meaner side of life with that lump on my head was a good thing. The entire scenario made me feel as though I needed to be tested, and I craved a right-of-passage that would be universally viewed by my circle of influence as *manly*. I needed something that would give me the adult credentials I so desperately sought. Despite evidence to the contrary, I completely bought into my father's idea that my siblings and I had all been given too much by my grandparents who were an integral part of our lives.

I can vividly recall him saying, "What are you going to do when your grandfather and grandmother aren't around anymore?" To me, that was a question of toughness. How was I going to survive in this hard-hitting world when I had no one to look out for me or shield me from the darker side of the world? My older brother was also an influence in my decision to pursue joining the Marines. He was approaching the age of eighteen, which required that he register for the United States Selective Service System, also known as "the draft."

The Vietnam War was going strong, and I was worried that my brother was going to be sent overseas. I remember making a solemn promise to myself: if my brother was not drafted to serve in the Vietnam War, when I was old enough, I would voluntarily choose to serve in one of the military branches.
I kept that promise.

I was tailored-made for the Corps. Everything conducted during training came with the pressure to do it right and do it very quickly. The first day of training was wildly chaotic, and July and August weather in Quantico, Virginia— the site of my training— was perpetually hot and humid. My love-hate relationship with the process started on day one of training. Sergeant instructors made it abundantly clear that they did not care whether any of us succeeded, and the environment was intentionally pressurized to make each of the two six-week increments feel like eternity. I can remember my first sergeant instructor telling me he was going to see to it that I was carried off "his" base on a gurney. He asked me, "What do you think about that, candidate?" Candidate is what all prospective officers are called and it was often spoken as if it were a pejorative. I responded very loudly, as all responses were expected to be given, "Sergeant Instructor, that is the only way *this candidate* is leaving this base!" I still believe he never expected such a response and will continue to believe I actually earned a measure of his respect with that response.

Succeeding and thriving in Officer Candidate School (OCS) became a test I set for myself. I needed to know that I could step up and handle the toughest challenges the Corps had to offer. Besides, the Marines allowed zero time for whining and feeling sorry for oneself, and not once did I hold a private pity party. Though I strongly disliked certain aspects of training, I fervently believed what we endured fully encompassed what it took to one day become a commissioned officer. Further, I felt the rigors of training needed to be hard because if it were easy, anyone could do it. I wanted to achieve something I felt might be on the edge of my capabilities. My internal gut reaction to the grit and gruel was to just get mad, but I woke up each day and gave the very best I had to offer. When I failed, I was only angry at myself because I constantly reminded myself that I was far from the first person to be challenged by the rigors of Marine Corps training.

During my first training increment, I hit a small stumbling block. I failed a written test and had to appear before a board. However, I never actually reached the board hearing stage. On my behalf, the commanding officer went before the board, briefed my case, and subsequently came out and instructed me to rejoin my fellow officer candidates in the squad bay. It was by far one of the best days of my life to date because there was the very real possibility of me having to repeat training, and on no level did I want to do that.

My gladiator mentality inspired me to never fail again, and in OCS, I did not.

At OCS, candidates were assigned "billets," which were standard jobs within a regular Marine Corps platoon. Our platoon commander was an absolute hard ass when it came to grading performance. I do not recall ever seeing him smile. He was a very short man, and anyone standing taller seemed to receive a bit more of his hostility. I was nine inches taller than him and tried not to stand close to him whenever possible. After holding a billet for a period of three days, one would receive one of three ratings: unsatisfactory, marginal, or satisfactory. I loved that the highest rating you could hope to get was *satisfactory*. The hell with a bunch of flowery language. When the Marines said you performed to a satisfactory level, that was damn high praise. At one point during training, I was selected to serve as Candidate Platoon Commander. There were three others who had held that billet prior to me and none had received a satisfactory rating.

I wanted that billet because it was the highest position within the platoon that an officer candidate could hold. You were responsible for the readiness, and to a lesser extent, the performance of your platoon. Of the three candidates previously mentioned, one or two let the billet go straight to their heads and barked out orders as though they were not going to be rejoining those same candidates three or four days later. I took note of their approach and developed a distinctively different style. I led by example and became a gladiator's gladiator.

If a fellow candidate needed help gathering their gear, I did not direct someone else to assist, I jumped in, and we completed the task together. I also worked hard to lead by persuasion and not authority, the latter of which was both limited and fleeting. In the end, when I was called before the platoon commander to receive my rating, I ran as fast as I could to his office. Under my leadership, the platoon performed well, but I suspected that no one was ever going to receive a satisfactory rating, including me.

When I reached the lieutenant's office, I banged on the hatch and loudly requested permission to enter. Permission was granted, and I stood at attention in front of his desk and practically shouted, "Candidate Mason reporting as ordered, Sir!" He laid the evaluation chit in front of me and told me to read it. Mind you, in OCS training, a candidate never picked up the chit and casually read. Absolutely not! You snapped your head down, took five seconds to read what you could and popped your head back up. All I saw when I looked down was the word *satisfactory* circled.

To this day, few ratings have made me as proud. I kept that chit for years after I completed training, but lost it in one of my many moves across my career. The Marine Corps taught me many life lessons, but among the most significant is the concept that when you believe you have reached your limit, you always have reserve in the tank. I have continued an array of different pursuits long after I simply wanted to quit; however, I always found myself glaring in the mirror with a realization that quitting would give me no safe harbor in which to evade the reality of my weakness.

Despite falling and failing at times and feeling as though I had no more energy, my time in the Marines as a young officer taught me that every form of gladiator just must dig a little bit deeper. Semper Fidelis!

The Federal Bureau of Investigation (FBI) was my next destination, and for 23 years, I served as special agent and ultimately advanced to the position of Executive Assistant Director, a position which was fourth on the FBI's food chain at the time. If you are worried that this book contains a two-decade account of how I helped nab the bad guys or put white-collar crooks in federal prisons, relax – it is not. Beginning with this first chapter, I sought to engage you with an array of stories that can be framed as anecdotes intended to convey a message related to confronting challenges head-on, smartly, and most importantly, effectively. In addition to obtaining my college degree and armed forces training, I embraced early lessons imparted by mentors, who I will introduce you to and share experiences that proved to be life-learned jewels.

I wanted to join the FBI from the time I was in seventh grade. I have always dreamed of more, and I had always wanted to work in law enforcement.

My childhood dream-track was to first join the Chicago Police Department, then the Illinois State Police, and then I decided to pursue appointment as an FBI Special Agent. I even authored a short story in our grade school paper about my FBI goals. I wish I had a single, defining moment that was the driver behind my quest to become a Special Agent, but the reality is a little less exciting. In the mid-1960s through the mid-70s, there was a television show called "The FBI," which starred Efrem Zimbalist, Jr. I loved that show! Back in those days, there was no ambiguity about good and evil as there is in so many of today's television features and movies. No slight to the name, title, or producers, but it appears the influence of urban series like "Power" entices millennials to pursue a street life hustle that defies law enforcement. Different influence, to say the very least.

Just about everyone in my neighborhood with whom I shared my dream dismissed it as not even remotely possible. Even my own stepmother told me, 'That's never going to happen,' but I was not swayed by negativity.

Never did I consider for a moment that I might have been fighting above my weight class. Although I shared my hopes and dreams with people I trusted as a young boy, I never let anyone dissuade me from goals I had set for myself. I am a relentless optimist and remained confident that I would succeed. I knew the FBI reviewed tens of thousands of applicants each year and always believed I would be one of the lucky selections. My appointment letter arrived in the mail one day prior to the end of my tour of duty with the Marines. Prior to that day, I was beginning to wonder if I was ever going to actually receive that coveted appointment letter. I had even begun to entertain thoughts of where my next professional arena was going to be. Thankfully, I never had to give that any further thought.

When I arrived at the FBI Academy—which is located on the same Marine Corps base where I went through my OCS training—my 20-week, intense training began. I felt comfortable interacting with my classmates, a group of young, accomplished individuals. I once again found myself quietly wondering if I had what it took to compete with this group. Perhaps an explanation is in order regarding the aforementioned nagging doubt. I attended

Medgar Evers Elementary School, a Chicago public grade school. I then successfully passed the entrance exam to attend Mendel Catholic Prep High School and looked forward to engaging in an academically challenging environment. However, from the first day of class, I felt as though I were playing catch-up with many of my high school classmates, most of whom had attended private Catholic grade schools. Classes that many of classmates considered "cake" courses were ones I struggled to successfully negotiate.

Approximately one-third of the way through New Agents' Training at the academy, I was confronted with a legitimate scare. There were two exams we had to take involving legal instruction: Legal I and Legal II. I failed Legal I, which was my first major setback since OCS.

I will not bore you with the details, but I had misread a question that was worth significant points, and I was incredibly angry at myself. The margin of error at the FBI Academy was small. A score of 84, which is the grade I received on the aforementioned exam, or below was considered failing, and two failures almost always meant dismissal from the Academy and the end of one's dream of becoming an FBI Special Agent. I decided to take a drive that day at the conclusion of classes. As I drove off campus, I momentarily pondered the idea that I was kidding myself. What if I was not the caliber of individual desired by the FBI for highly sought-after special agent positions? Is there a chance that I do not belong here? I am guessing I had not rolled ten more yards before slamming my hand on the dashboard of my car and exclaiming, "I absolutely belong here, and I will take that test again and knock it out of the park!" I, along with five of my classmates, sat for the retest Friday morning of the same week at 7:00 a.m. before the start of the day's regular course of instruction. I scored a 99% and desperately wanted to know where I had lost a point, but decided it was time to just move on.

As a young agent I worked general crimes, but also worked several undercover assignments targeting drug dealers. I eventually rose to become one of the three highest ranking Black Special

14

Agents in FBI history; there has since been one other Black agent promoted to the position of Executive Assistant Director (EAD).

Regardless of the arena, a gladiator spirit is defined by one's indomitable will to win. I harbored a leadership state of mind, and I never reached the finish line by paying close attention to my perceived limitations or untimely stumbles.

My only barrier was my own thinking, and I will always be proud of the fact that I did not let that initial exam failure persuade me to cut my losses and leave the academy on my own accord. No way! If I was going to be denied my lifelong dream of becoming an FBI Special Agent, I was going to leave dirty, bloodied, and not without giving it my absolute best effort. There are few things more satisfying than stepping into the arena, standing on the precipice of failure, and emerging victorious. I had long before decided that I was going attack my professional life with the spirit of a gladiator, never yielding to my own self-doubts. I must momentarily digress here to make a small point. When I played Little League baseball, I was never a good hitter. However, I felt with absolute certainty that every time I stepped up to the plate, I was going to bash that ball far into the outfield. That actually happened very rarely, as most of the balls I swung at landed safely in the catcher's mitt. Against all evidence to the contrary, I have always had faith in myself. As with many people, my biggest adversary existed in my own self-doubts that the gladiator spirit would eventually lay to rest. No, I never became a good, reliable hitter, but I never approached the plate thinking, "Well, here we go again, I'll never hit this guy." I thought exactly the opposite… every time.

I retired from my final professional arena after serving as senior vice-president and chief security officer for Verizon Communications, Inc., a Fortune 20 company. If you think I have conquered every obstacle that three separate employment sectors can offer, think again. I have not, but I opted to share my life's examples with the intent of illustrating practical, real-life examples along with strategies for effectively managing a variety of workplace situations. Throughout my tenure as an executive, I have too often heard of people complaining about one aspect or another of their employment. When asked, "What have you done to address the situation?" far too many have responded, "What can I, one person with no influence, possibly do?" I have also heard employees and colleagues alike vigorously complain about an incident that occurred within their place of employment, but when an all-hands gathering was held and executives asked for questions or comments, nothing came forth from individuals who were previously foaming at the mouth regarding a workplace situation they found intolerable.

A seasoned spectator will often complain endlessly but pass on any opportunity to raise the subject in a forum with individuals who actually have the authority to address the complaint. Feel as though your workplace lacks diversity? Are you someone who actively recruits externally and internally to diversify your team or company? Are you suggesting better methods to reach out to relevant stakeholders like racial and gender minorities, or members of the LGBTQ community? What is the current level of tolerance in your workplace?

Have you made it abundantly clear that homophobic or racist jokes are not welcomed in your professional arena?

We get to decide every day of the week the role we will play in shaping the world in which we exist. Can one person change the dynamics within their environment single-handedly? Not likely, but we can all contribute a variety of positive ways, including our influence on one person at a time. In all fairness, the American workforce can represent serious white-water rapids for both spectators and gladiators. We all must continue to work hard to eliminate such negative impacts, but what about you and your journey right now—today? How do you navigate *those* white-water rapids to pave your path for success? Among the stories you will read hereafter is one that centers around an unconscious bias and in which I am the antagonist. It is a story about a hero's refusal to be treated in a second-class manner and my own awakening to the pitfalls of unconscious bias. I worked diligently from that point forward to recognize and acknowledge this bias-factor in all matters forward (More on the actual story later). It is a winning example of a gladiator spirit; someone determined to no longer tolerate biases impacting her career.

The war on all the ills that afflict our society is not going to be won by a single person, but by the aggregate of thousands of inputs from all manner of people. It is a give and give relationship and not give and take. We cannot have it both ways, i.e., wishing for a better world, but doing nothing to make that world a reality.

This book is a call to step-up and be a part of the solution. Spectator or gladiator? Only you can decide which title fits your path. What matters is not the title per se, but your acknowledgment of who and what you intend to be in your professional life.

Chapter Two

Raised by a Village

"Remember, there is always time to do the job right the second time."

-Audrey Wright

The titles selected for the first two chapters of this book might strike some readers as contradictory. How can I simultaneously be a man who has often felt as though he stood alone on an island, yet proclaim to have been raised by a village? I have listened to my contemporaries complain about racism or being mistreated by those in authority and often wondered how so few such incidents ever touched my life. I have wondered aloud why I have never felt the anger of some of my friends. Finally, I wondered why I feel, even to this day, that the impact of racism on my life has been minimal. Was my innate optimism a form of denial? Writing this book produced the answer I believe most accurately reflects my views on life and why I have so seldom felt the impact of racism in my own life. There is a larger explanation in the chapter titled, "This World Owes You Nothing."

It is my father to whom I attribute many of the characteristics that have made me the man I am today. Several of my neighbors, many of whom were an integral part of my life as a young boy growing up on the Southside of Chicago, are also responsible for molding the man I was to become. A common characteristic possessed by all the significant individuals who either considerably impacted my life, or to whom I gravitated, was that none suffered excuses well. They were blue-collared Black men and women who were first-time homeowners in our neighborhood. They had moved from sad and depressing housing projects to owning their own single-family homes. They were construction workers, city workers, postal employees and held varied other jobs. Most importantly, they were enormously proud people who enjoyed a middle-class life that included the ownership of automobiles, homes, and for some, even modest vacation properties.

Additionally, my neighbors served as my teachers and mentors who focused on ensuring that the neighborhood children were positioned to pursue opportunities they were denied in their own lives.

The originating elders I refer to as my village suffered racial indignities on the job and in their daily lives that were common in their time, but none that I ever experienced in my own life. Their opportunities were more limited than my own and some of the stories they shared told of the challenges they believed I too, would experience as I stepped out into the world. However, I began the process of deciding how my life's journey would take shape without any trepidation or fear based on stories they shared with me about their own journeys through life. I would be remiss if I did not state that my life and that of my peers have not been without struggles. I have just never felt comfortable complaining when I know of the struggles those who preceded me routinely faced. I had witnessed firsthand that the limited opportunities for so many who preceded me did not even touch the perimeter of the vast prospects the world availed to me. While I may not have been on equal footing with the majority world, I had far fewer, if any, limitations artificially injected into my life as did many of the members of the village that raised me.

As I reflect on my youth, most of the people that I gravitated towards were privy to the pain and frustrations of segregation in ways that I had read about in school, but for the most part, had never experienced in my own life.

I was further fortunate enough to be told compelling stories by them, some of which contain details that were haunting. I have never been denied a seat in a restaurant or told where to sit on a bus or train. I have never been denied a hotel room and never once had to consider with a cautious heart where I stopped to secure lodging while traveling. My village elders clawed and fought hard to become the first in their families to pursue higher education, which in some instances included both high school and vocational school (college for most was still out of reach). They knew what it meant to be denied promotions, or even worse, to never be considered for advancement. I could never give an accurate count of how many times I heard the phrase, "It's a hard world out there" whenever I engaged in a conversation with the elders of my village.

None of their stories or warnings ever compelled me to change the view of my own life's planned trajectory. I must admit upon reflection that I don't know if I was genuinely bold or just plain naïve. I know I felt so motivated by their stories that I knew I didn't want to have any similar stories to tell my children one day. Despite hearing stories of how unfairly many of my neighbors and relatives had been treated at work, I nevertheless started working without any apprehension believing that I would be treated in accordance with my performance. I have embraced this idea throughout my professional life and though some may doubt me, I have rarely been disappointed. These influential neighbors were also my life's early bosses who were tough whenever I was recruited or asked to complete small jobs for them.

The village that unknowingly fostered my early gladiator spirit were so much more than mere bosses. These were people who wholeheartedly cared about me. My future was their priority, and they collectively invested time and precious resources in me.

I was always an eager and willing student but I will not engage in revisionist history by suggesting I always knew they were giving me invaluable lessons that could not be taught in a classroom. I cannot pretend now that I always appreciated being paid so little for performing what I considered hard, dirty, and demanding work. Nonetheless, I loved having my own money and rarely asked my father for funds, which was quite frankly a good thing since he was not inclined to open his wallet for recreational activities such as movies, bowling, or outings at amusement parks. I can barely recall asking for much of anything after I turned nine or ten years old, and that included necessities such as new school clothes.

Prior to working at my first check-paying job, I completed odd jobs for many of my neighbors, but worked most consistently for my next-door neighbor, Audrey Wright. Audrey— who insisted we call her "Audrey" and not Mrs. Wright— epitomized a serious, hardworking, self-made woman. Most of the adults who resided on the block where I was raised were in their mid-thirties to early-forties. Audrey was in her mid-fifties and reminded me of my grandmother and was someone in my life I loved like I loved my grandmother.

My biological mother passed away following a hard-fought battle with Lupus before I reached the age of two. As mentioned, my father remarried and my stepmother lived with us for a short span of time, but it was Audrey who was one of the most influential role models of my childhood and young adulthood.

Her three children were older than most of the other kids on the block and had reached adulthood by the time I reached the age of ten. To know Audrey was to love her as she had a heart as big as all outdoors, but could be perceived as stern to those who did not know her well. Audrey was all business when it came to assigning me even ridiculously small jobs. She held a professional job as a World Book Encyclopedia salesperson prior to the advent of the internet. I believed her to be one of the most determined and successful individuals I had ever encountered.

Audrey was a visionary who was eventually promoted to the position of regional manager, an appointment rarely reserved for women, especially black women, during the 1960s. I believe she succeeded by sheer force-of-personality alone and didn't care what anyone thought. She would go straight for your heart if you said the wrong thing to her, and one never had to worry about where she stood on any issue. When her husband, Bob, wanted to have a garage built, I overheard the conversation they had with the representative of the contracted company. It was not Bob who did most of the negotiation, but rather Audrey who stressed the importance of quality workmanship—fit and finish. Furthermore, she exhibited unabashed boldness when she stated that she would be watching with an eagle's eye for anything subpar in the workmanship and construction of their new garage. She also boldly told the salesman that she expected the same comparable quality his company provided to people in *other* neighborhoods.

On another occasion, I overheard when she spoke to a customer about buying a set of encyclopedias. Such a purchase was a significant financial expenditure for the average Black family in our neighborhood, but Audrey's point-of-view did not focus on just an encyclopedia purchase. She viewed it as an investment in a child's education. She was prepared to compare the price of this *investment* with all manner of other purchases families routinely made that offered nothing beyond a bit of instant gratification. Audrey could shame the most reluctant client into folding and agreeing to allow her to close a sale when I suspected that they would have never done so with a less determined salesperson. On several occasions, I accompanied her on sales calls with potential customers. Despite her commanding presence, it never occurred to me that she was using high pressure tactics to sell books. Audrey may have been my first introduction to a gladiator tactic that utilized the talent of analysis and persuasion rather than a sword and shield!

I choose to not consider myself an early spectator but a gladiator in training as I continuously witnessed how Audrey passionately persuaded potential customers with the genuine passion she exhibited for the product she sold.

Despite her savvy, I found myself wanting to temporarily disappear as she skillfully shredded any resistance to the logic of her sales pitch. I almost felt sorry for some of the customers who had invited Audrey into their homes. They had no idea of the force of personality they were about to meet! Audrey presented an overwhelmingly convincing argument and then pierced her

22

potential client with a stare that dared a response. She genuinely found it hard to believe that anyone would not want to buy such a treasured set of books for their children. She was eventually promoted to manager, led other teams of salespeople, and succeeded because she believed in both herself and the value of her product. Audrey wanted to see young Black children gain access to every advantage possible as they pursued their life's ambitions.

Audrey was focused, absolutely driven, and successful; I wanted to grow up to be the same.

My most admired village-mentor (Audrey) was the type of person to be avoided if you knew she was doing something like moving and you had no intention of tying up your weekend to help her move. Responding with an affirmative "No" to Audrey was not an option. As with all I learned by watching her engaged in her craft, no detail was insignificant when I worked for Audrey, and she expected my performance to measure up to her strict standards. The fact that I was an eager nine-year-old boy when I first began working for her hardly seemed to matter. I can remember the very first time I mopped and waxed her kitchen floor. I was about eleven at the time, but again, my age for Audrey was not a mitigating factor relative to the quality of work she expected from me. If she was going to pay me for a job, all that mattered was that the results met her standards. Her kitchen floor was covered in an old, dark-green tile that was popular at the time. It was time to get to work.

The kitchen floor was the type of floor that required a liquid wax application to achieve a nice, shiny luster. Her kitchen was small, but everything had its own place. The room's aesthetic required that the open area achieve a polished finished that was complementary. So, after finishing many other chores, I was ready to tackle the kitchen floor. Audrey provided minimal instructions; she just told me to get started. I both mopped and dried the floor and then worked feverishly to polish it. However, after I finished giving what I thought was the last tile an impressive sheen, I realized that I did not get to a corner of the floor that was under the table and abutted two walls of the kitchen.

To reach the unwaxed area, I was going to have to move the table which most assuredly was going to scratch a substantial portion of the work I had just completed, and from my vantage point, looked rather good. I had already put away everything I had used to complete this task and felt my little oversight would never be caught. Wrong! The first place Audrey looked was under the table. She asked me one single question: "Honey, did you wax that corner under the table?" I told her that I had not, and she told me that I needed to get it done for the job to be considered complete. She then told me that I would have to repolish areas that were going to be scratched when I moved the table.

Audrey paused, looked me in the eye and said, 'Remember, there is always time to do the job right the second time.' The lesson? Do it right the first time.

Audrey did not care that it was a beautiful summer day, nor did she factor into the equation that a few of my friends had already asked if I had finished working. None of that mattered. What did matter was that we had an agreement, and I had yet to live up to my end of the bargain: simple, straightforward, and no wiggle room for excuses.

Audrey taught me how to properly complete a small job, and she also effectively taught me that every job —no matter how seemingly insignificant— was to be done properly. This early lesson served as a framework for my future in the professional arena.

Once I became eligible to receive a real, check-paying job, I jumped at the opportunity. My first opportunity was at an independently owned gas station called Gas U.S.A., located at 95th and Vincennes. I landed that position with a recommendation from my father. The owner's name was Marion Favors, and though I'd never previously met Marion, he and my father had apparently been friends for some time. One day my father was at the station and Marion—who was widely known as "Fat Boy"— had bemoaned the fact that he could not find good help to work the pumps while he tended to other business at the station. My father told Marion that he had a 15-year-old son who could help him. Marion responded, "Mason, I don't want any young kids working here." My father quipped that I was not an average kid like the others and assured him that I was a responsible young man.

I reached the age of thirty-five before I heard my father say he was proud of me, but I had been told stories by other people that he was indeed quite proud.

I did not learn of the conversation he and Marion held until one year later, when the station was about to close for the final time. The "gas crisis" of the mid-70s, along with extremely poor business practices, had squeezed Marion out of business. It was such a sad day when we shut off the lights for the final time in December of 1974. The station had represented far more than just a job to me. I was in the daily company of (mostly) men, all of whom had something to teach me about life. I was at that impressionable age when a young boy tried to define what it meant to be a man, and I had worked in an environment that afforded me access to many role models. Some were good and some not-so-good.

When I first met Marion, he told me he was skeptical of my ability to handle the job but offered that he would give me a shot if I passed his interview process, which was not to be conducted in a comfortable room that made me feel relaxed. The interview took place while he engaged in the work of running his small business. I immediately knew that Marion was a genuinely nice man, but he had a fledging gas station to run and needed to know that I could run the pumps and master other necessary tasks to successfully complete a day of work. Even though I knew I was being tested for my position, he never made me feel uneasy. He fixed cars, managed financial books, ordered inventory, and tended to a host of other duties. He was a short man and a bit overweight but possessed a very easygoing manner. Marion was also a quick wit and funny.

There were occasions when he would ask me what I would like for lunch because he was going to pick up lunch for himself while away running errands. If I asked, "How much does a sandwich and chips cost?" he fired back, "If you must ask, you can't afford it!" Actually, he never made me pay him back when he bought my lunch.

Marion's gas station was a precursor to today's modern gas stations that serve as multipurpose convenience stores, where patrons can practically shop for a week's worth of groceries. Gas U.S.A. sold milk, eggs, cigarettes, and a limited assortment of basic auto supplies, and this was long before the existence of debit and credit cards. This was a pure cash and carry business, so being able to solve basic math problems with speed was an essential qualification for the job. So, Marion posed potential problems to me such as the following: he initially told me the price of eggs, milk, and cigarettes and then proceeded to query me regarding some or all the above. For example, a customer bought $7 in gas (a sum that filled most tanks at a time when gas was 29 cents a gallon), two dozen eggs, a gallon of milk, and a pack of cigarettes. The customer gives you a $2 How much change do you owe the customer? Marion asked me these questions while I followed him around the station and filled customers' gas tanks or performed other work. There was no time to grab a pencil and a pad. More importantly, there was not any expectation that I would need such tools. Fortunately, I had learned to add quickly by going bowling with my father. After every roll of his ball, he would want to know his possible score in the next frame, and almost immediately after he released his ball, he'd then want to know his current score. My father was many things, but patient was not among them. I would literally create four scoring scenarios, starting with him knocking down six pins, all the way through scoring a strike. He always knocked down six pins, so I thought that was a good place to start. Once I computed his score using six pins as my base, anything else just required me to add a few more numbers. Automatic scorers did not exist in those days and scores were kept manually on a scorecard designed for bowling.

I imagine most young people today who do not bowl on a regular basis have zero knowledge of how bowling is scored because of automatic scorers. Marion would have had no issue at all telling me I could not work for him, so I knew I needed to be as quick with my answers to him as I was with the bowling scores I kept for my father. It was a simple proposition: pass his little math tests or go back to other summertime pursuits. As it happened, I worked for Marion for just under one year. In addition to working 40 hours a week during the summer, I also worked every weekend for him during the school year.

One additional demand Marion made of me during the summer months was to meet him at his house and ride with him to the station. He lived less than a mile from my house, so I could walk to his house, ring the doorbell, and wait for him to answer the door. He hustled to finish getting ready, and as he opened the door for me to come inside and wait for him, I always smelled soap and aftershave as he hurriedly rushed past me getting ready to head into work. There was something comforting about the consistency with which our mornings began. I was never treated like a child, but as a young man. I was once more being taught the importance of basic components of success: being reliable and being on time.

Once Marion finished dressing, we would climb into his car and drive roughly two miles to the station. We would talk about the day ahead and any special jobs he had for me. Although it only took a few minutes to cover the distance between his home and the station, I loved those conversations. He made me feel as though I was part of his circle of confidants and that, too, made me feel like a man. When he first assigned the additional responsibility of meeting him at his home, Marion told me, "I need you at my door at 5:00 a.m. I don't need you on the way at 5:00 a.m., I need you at my door!" I was never late, not even once. I share this fact not to brag about such a simple thing, but rather to convey how yet another person in my village didn't want to hear any excuses regarding the failure to execute on an agreed upon job.

I was a sophomore in high school when Gas U.S.A. closed. As I mentioned above, the station was a casualty of the so-called "gas crisis" (circa 1974-75) and the fact that Marion was a poor businessman. His kindness proved to be his undoing. He had customers who ran up tabs exceeding $600. That may not sound like a huge figure today, but this is when gas was less than thirty cents per gallon! Then, he would let some of his debtors *work off* their debt by pumping gas. First, this *work* was always performed when I was there. Second, as these debtors were all grown men, most did extraordinarily little actual work as I hustled to run from one customer to the next. Finally, he would pay these individuals $6.50 an hour when I was being paid $2 an hour. The debt Marion carelessly allowed to run amok eventually impaired his revenue stream to the degree that he was forced to shut down the business. He could no longer afford to pay for a truckload of gas, and his suppliers were not nearly as kind with their customers as Marion was with his. I loved that job and the camaraderie I felt with the men and women I came to know from working at the station. It was, and remains, a special chapter of my life.

After the station closed, I found myself in need of another job, and preferably one that paid more than $2 an hour because I was aware that I needed to start saving money for college. The entire cost of my college education was to be handled by me. I knew I was not going to receive any assistance from my father or any other relative. So, it was time to find a better paying job. I had hoped to find work at Jewel Food Stores, a place I had seen young teenagers work and knew was a decent job. It was also one that included premium pay for working Sundays and holidays. There was a new Jewel Food Store being built at 87Th and State Street, and it was to be a Jewel *Grand Bazaar,* complete with thirty-four checkout lanes and considered to be the largest store in Chicago!

I was late applying for a job there and felt incredibly lucky when I was hired as a bag boy. The general manager of the store was a Black woman named Essie Boyd, and she was someone I was immediately impressed by because she reminded me of one of my grade-school teachers. She dressed in business attire every day, and her hair was always put up in a tight bun, not unattractive, but clearly intended as part of her overall business-first persona. Her glasses were low fashion and always hung around her neck. She seemed to be in perpetual motion, much like a professional football coach who constantly moves up and down the field, pushing his players to find the next higher level of play. She moved around the store constantly, and if she was passing through your area of responsibility, she was going to let you know if something needed to be fixed. Mrs. Boyd was positive as well and not reserved about complimenting employees, but she was never given to casual conversations. She was to become another part of my extended village.

Once she addressed approximately forty young and brand-new employees the day before the store opened and had only one thing to tell us. Mrs. Boyd said, "Boys, if you want to continue working here, I have only one demand (not a *request*): never let me see you standing still. It is not my job to constantly tell you what to do nor find something for you to do. Rather, it is your job to be constantly looking for something to do." End of the discussion. Some of the boys were clearly concerned and looked as though this might not be the job for them, but not me.

I had been "raised" as a worker by all the people in my neighborhood. I embraced her directive and thought that she did not need to give me that warning because she was never going to see me standing still. After the store opened, crowds were initially enormous as people traveled from far away neighborhoods just to see the store rumored to be larger than any other store in the Chicago area. I quickly realized that the store initially hired more employees than it needed to ensure every customer had a positive experience in their initial visits to the store. There were times when business was slow and many of the young boys were standing around doing nothing. Only days earlier, we had been advised that this behavior was not the way to guarantee our continued employment. Having been hired later than most of the other boys, I worried that if store management started reducing staff, I would be among the first to be let go.

As a result, I doubled down on ensuring that I was always in motion. I either wiped down counters, restocked paper bags, cleaned up after customers or helped the other boys on their lanes.

Several of the older teenagers asked me why I worked so hard and even suggested that I was trying to win the favor of Mrs. Boyd. I assured them I was merely doing what I was supposed to be doing and defiantly stated that I was furthermore doing what I was being paid to do. I was getting paid for four hours of work (average shift), and I intended to work for each of those four hours. I never had an issue with Mrs. Boyd's warning to us because, again, I never intended on doing anything less. I have no doubt she has been described by some using less-than-charitable adjectives, but she was exactly what I expected of a "boss."

She was never mean; I never heard her disrespect anyone and I never heard her raise her voice. Mrs. Boyd told you exactly what she expected and made it quite clear what the consequences would be if you failed to live up to her expectations.

The words she chose were never threatening but made clear the agreement we all needed to understand.

She was so much more than just a boss and let it be known that part of her job was to raise the next generation of managers. Although she was unbothered by having to exercise her authority, I always felt she preferred to lead through persuasion. She wanted us to know what high quality work demanded and that nothing she asked of us was beyond our capability.

After approximately two months, the curiosity factor started to fade as customers came to understand that the store was larger than any others in the city, but essentially offered no more than their local grocery stores. The opening day sales and giveaways started to fade, which eliminated any special benefit to shopping at the store. I also imagined that the longer drive to get there no longer made sense and the crowds became less spectacular, especially during the week. As I predicted, management eliminated some of the staff. By that time, I had already been moved to the parcel pick-up island and was working more hours each shift. Some of the boys, many of whom had been hired before me, were terminated. They were, perhaps, the first spectators I had witnessed who partially caused their own demise.

My boss on the parcel pick-up island was an assistant manager named Willie Bradley. Willie was an intense, stern, and demanding man, but a magnificent manager. He was a 30-year-old Black man who, at least initially, never appeared the least concerned as to whether he was *liked* by his small staff. At times he seemed unnecessarily gruff. I now believe Willie himself was learning how to be an effective leader and gladiator in his own right. He clearly had ambitions far beyond managing the parcel pick-up island and knew management had little tolerance for sloppy work or lazy employees.

He was eventually promoted to manage the frozen food section and took me with him. By now I was an 18-year-old high school senior. One day, I casually mentioned to Willie that I was due to receive my first quarter grades the following week. I have never forgotten the brief conversation with Willie that immediately followed my casual utterance:

Me: "I guess I'll be getting my first-quarter grades next week."

Willie: "When you get your grades, I want to see them."

(I did not actually respond, but my face must have given my thoughts away.)

Willie: "I know what you are thinking. I am not your father and have no right to see your grades. However, you are going to do more than work in this frozen foods section. You were meant for bigger things. I do not want this job becoming a distraction to you. If your grades are not good, I won't have you working for me."

That was it. The entire conversation. No rebuttal, no whining or even suggesting that I was not going to show him my report card. I brought Willie my report card the following week. In fact, as I was due to work the evening of the same day that I received my grades, Willie was the first person to see them. I have shared

31

this story with many audiences in my adulthood during speaking engagements, but the first few times I shared it, my eyes welled with tears. I had friends whose parents did not care about their grades, and here was someone I initially perceived as completely disinterested in my grades telling me that not only was there more for me in this world, but also that my current job was not going to be the reason I did not rise to my potential. Willie mentioned to me on several occasions that he believed that I had a bright future. I always believed he meant within the company as almost all the managers started "in the front of the store" as cashiers or bag boys. He spoke to me about managing a store as large as the one we both worked in and even managing one district or more. Willie saw basic things such as showing up on time and being reliable as a few of the keys to success that I'd already mastered, but his confidence in me was a driver behind my performance while working for him.

I have long awoken with a deep sense of gratitude for the quality of men and women, more of whom you will read about, who constantly pushed me in the right direction.

These people range from those mentioned in this chapter to teachers who saw capabilities in me that I did not see in myself. They included a neighbor who called me over to his porch after hearing me swearing on the basketball court just across the street from his house. I remember that he asked me, "Michael, how would your father like to know how you were cursing out there just now?" I apologized profusely for my language, promised he would never hear me talk like that again and then prayed my apology would be sufficient to keep him from any further need to share my transgressions with my dad.

He did not feel the need to tell on me, but I never ever carelessly cursed on those courts again. I must write *carelessly* because anything else would be less than completely honest. However, I do believe every time I subsequently allowed an unfettered F-bomb to come out of my mouth, my eyes immediately diverted to his porch to ensure he was not sitting there watching me violate my promise to him. As a young boy I lived to please people. The combination of people believing in me and my desire to please them proved to be a good recipe for trying, as I still do now, to constantly improve the person I am today.

Chapter Three

The World Owes You Nothing

"Boy, come over here. I am going to show you how to iron a shirt *one time,* and I don't want to see you in another shirt that wrinkled ever again."

-My father, the late Howard G. Mason

As I considered the chapters to include in this book, I decided to move this one closer to the beginning due to something my father said to me many times as I was growing up:

"Boy, remember this, the world owes you nothing."

On numerous occasions, my father spoke those dynamic words to me, and it helped shape my perspective on this world, including how I would both approach and interpret those things that I would consider unfair. There are many injustices in this world, and most have existed since the dawn of time. There are injustices within the judicial system, public education, the workplace—literally everywhere the quest for a productive and successful life occurs.

Akin to the trailblazers from chapter 2 who served as my life's early mentors, there have been heroes like Thurgood Marshall, whose influence carved pathways for a criminal justice and legal system that would strive to provide racial equity and rule on cases like Brown vs. The Board of Education, which desegregated schools across America. In the process, we learned that it is just and right to maintain a consistent front against such injustices in a quest to make the world and—closer to home—our country, a fair, equitable, and inclusive environment.

Civilizations have always found ways to separate the chosen from all others and elevate them while mistreating those deemed of lesser value. The road to success is not paved equally for all. I am not referring to the benefits derived from doing demanding work in a superior manner. Rewards *should* flow to those whose dedication and hard work have made them masters of their craft. As a society, we speak often of the unequal distribution of wealth, status, and position residing at the highest level within corporations. I believe it is necessary to distinguish between the rewards reaped through hard work and those reaped as a result of other factors. The focus should be on the differential in opportunities that provide each of us with the tools to reach our greatest potential. Everyone is not going to be afforded a leadership position in the name of equality. Nor are high paying executive jobs, senior status in the military, doctoral degrees or any other generally accepted symbols of success going to be distributed to ensure there is equal representation in each of the aforementioned communities based upon gender, race, religion, or sexual preferences. Essentially, we are not all going to be provided with the tools that make the road to success equally accessible.

The injustice phenomenon did not begin yesterday, and it will not end tomorrow. So, what do we do in the face of this reality today? None of us can afford to wait for someone else to set the table for us.

We can ill-afford to wait until the tools lending themselves to a successful career are equally distributed. We cannot wait to be invited to participate in our dream career because it is dominated by people who do not look, act, or worship as we do.

As I will repeatedly assert throughout this book, I have been an active mentor for most of my adult life. I have heard many of my mentees lament the way they have been treated, or worse, expect to be treated. I parenthetically wrote the word "worse" for the latter characterization because I believe the anticipation of being treated in a particular manner can lead to behavior that results in a self-fulfilling prophecy.

For example, if you *think* your race, gender, color, religion, or sexual preference is going to impact the way you are going to be received or heard in the classroom or during a business meeting, you might—with no confirming evidence—decide to withhold your remarks rather than deal with the outcome you have already decided is most probable. Let me state for the record that I do not care whether there is confirming evidence for how you anticipate being treated, i.e., another colleague of the same gender, race, religion, nationality, or rank was treated poorly in a similar setting, so I am going to remain silent lest I receive the same treatment. Therein lies the recipe for a self-fulfilling prophecy. For every advancement that has been made in any type of professional relationship, *someone* has to be bold enough to engage and challenge conventional wisdom. Every time I invited team members of disparate ranks to the table for a discussion, I opened the discussion by telling everyone seated at the table that I wanted to hear their input. I went beyond this request and would ask for input from individuals I either knew had something important to offer or just to hear what they were thinking.

If you cave in to *anticipated resistance,* then you have no space to complain about the outcome of situations in which you had the opportunity to engage. Let me share one of my favorite stories to make my point clear. As you will see, if you have not already discovered, I believe in using simple, straightforward, real-life stories to convey important points. The following aligns, but understand the story is not subjectively about football, but rather football served in the moment as the perfect analogy to the point I was making for the audience below:

I was once asked to give the "commencement address" to a group of young boys who were graduating from a 4-week science-focused day camp sponsored by the company I worked for at the time. I opened by telling the boys a bit of my own history. I went on to say that I believed it was critical for them to understand the difference

36

between dreams and goals. I told them that we wish for the former and work for the latter.

I wanted them to understand the need to embrace the sacrifice, focus, and commitment it takes to succeed in any endeavor at the highest level. I further conveyed that I hoped some of them would one day work as engineers or as computer specialists for my company. However, I told them I hope one or more of them might one day start or lead a company that competed with my company.

Perhaps one of them would invent something that would greatly impact the lives of others. I told the boys they were the primary controllers of their future, much of which was limited only by their imagination, passion, commitment, and willingness to make sacrifices today for the downrange benefits such efforts are bound to yield tomorrow.

Then, something remarkably interesting occurred. One of the camp counselors, a 20-year-old rising college sophomore, raised his hand and said, "Mr. Mason, you can't possibly be telling these boys all they have to do is be focused and work hard and they will achieve all of their desires. There are other factors which often control outcomes which are beyond our ability to control." He sat back convinced his challenge to me would have me responding in a generic, non-specific manner. I felt badly that someone as young as him was already convinced his path to success had more relevant determinants than his will to succeed. How much practical or *actual* experience could he have amassed at such an early age beyond stories he had read or things he had heard? How much actual personal experience could he have gained in this arena at such a young age? This is precisely what I was referring to earlier in this book: the premature decision that the world views you differently and therefore your goals must be modified, pursued differently, tapered down a bit, or released altogether. Outrageous! My response used a simple illustration intended to make a powerful point.

I would like to reference the young man's question as I share more of our conversation. I told him I was making no such claim that the path to success would not be littered with various obstacles of one sort or another. At that moment, I decided to change course and make my point in a manner all present could easily understand. Remember, my targeted audience were ten to thirteen-year-old boys in the program; however, I also wanted to touch the young men who were working as counselors. I asked the assembled audience by the show of hands how many had ever played football. Roughly half the boys enthusiastically raised their hands. Then I asked how many had played the position of running back and a smaller number raised their hands.

I very intentionally called on the youngest boy I could find. I asked that young boy the following question, "When the football is snapped and handed off to you, what are you trying to do?"

He replied that he was trying to score a touchdown. I then asked, "What do the eleven boys on the other side of the line of scrimmage want to do after the ball is handed off to you?" He responded saying they wanted to tackle him and stop him from getting to the goal line. I asked whether that fact made him curl up in a fetal position on the ground and cry? He quite naturally and vigorously responded "No!" I then asked, "Did those eleven boys intent on stopping him cause him to run up into the stands?" I received the same vigorous response along with the same high level of intensity. Finally, I asked, "Okay, there are eleven boys trying very hard to stop you from reaching the goal line. So, what does that make you do?"

Folks, this exchange was completely unrehearsed. I had no idea how he was going to respond to my final question, but his response made me want to go up and hug him. He responded—and this is an exact quote from an 11-year-old boy— "It makes me work harder to get across the goal line." I looked at the 20-year-old counselor, who asked the question leading to this exchange, and said, "That is what I am telling all of you today. Life will present you with many different obstacles as you pursue the goals you hope to achieve. So what?"

We should focus on ridding society of obstacles that have nothing to do with our intelligence, capabilities, desire, ambition, or any other credible asset that does matter, but we cannot wait until society has succeeded in attaining that lofty goal.

However, the young running back understood that the obstacles presented by those eleven boys on the other side of the line of scrimmage were a challenge, but they did not unilaterally determine the outcome of each play nor the energy or focus he could apply to overcome those challenges–as it is with all of us. We will be confronted with obstacles–nothing new there. Most of us have relatively small cheering sections to turn to when confronted with such obstacles. In the moment, much like my young running back friend, we are on our own. None of that should matter. What matters is how hard we are willing to work to overcome those obstacles. If we fold our metaphorical goals tent and put it away, who do we have to blame? To me, it is about controlling what you can control and then forging ahead.

I learned at a very young age that obstacles to success merely required an increase in one's focus to overcome. When I was in the third grade, I came downstairs wearing a very wrinkled flannel shirt. My father—a single parent at the time who was raising three children—took one look at me and said, "Boy, come over here. I am going to show you how to iron a shirt *one time,* and I don't want to see you in another shirt that wrinkled ever again." All I knew about irons is that they got very hot and could burn me instantly if touched in the wrong spot. I was intimidated by the hot iron, but was more intimidated by my father's admonition that I was never again to be seen in a shirt as wrinkled as the one I was wearing when my one and only ironing lesson commenced.

It didn't matter to my father that I had to stand on a box to iron my shirt at the age of nine, nor did he concern himself with the potential danger of having a child so young use an iron. He figured if I could understand his instructions, I was smart enough to not burn myself—at least not twice—using the iron.

I listened intently as my father gave me those ironing instructions. I had no sense of the impropriety of having a boy so young iron his own clothes and still iron my shirts today exactly as my father instructed me over 55 years ago. Heck, I also iron my dress shirts after retrieving them from the local cleaners. Hey, have you seen a shirt from the dry cleaners? The sleeves are an afterthought! They make my work easier, but I almost never wear a shirt brought directly from the cleaners. I hope my father is looking down on me with a smile on his face because he created in me a desire to never show up anywhere looking unkempt. I digress.

There is yet another story that led me to respond to "incidents" that happened to me when I was a young boy in a manner much different than most. My teeth were very crooked in my youth, and I really wanted braces.

After I graduated from 8th grade and was headed to high school, I asked my father if I could get braces. His exact words were, "We can see the orthodontist next week. I will ask him how much your braces will cost. Once you give me one-third of that amount, you can get braces."

My father did not concern himself with the answer to the question of how much those highly desired braces might cost, which in turn might have had him reconsider what he was asking his young son to do. He made me an offer that was not open for discussion. It was both the best offer and the only offer I was to receive. I had absolutely no idea how much orthodontic treatment would cost, so my ignorance of the subject was an unlikely ally. Had I known the cost of braces prior to my appointment, I might have prematurely decided I could never raise my portion of the overall cost.

We scheduled an appointment with an orthodontist for the following week. The orthodontist took an impression of my teeth and then called me and my father into his office. He told my father that I would have to wear braces for close to four years and went onto explain what would occur through the duration of that time. My father essentially had only one interest in that conversation,

40

and that was the cost of my braces. The orthodontist presented the total cost: $2,100. Right there in the doctor's office, my father looked at me and said, "Boy (I should have advised earlier that "Boy" was a term of endearment from my father and always spoken with love), when you give me $700, we can make an appointment to start having your braces put on."

I have no idea whether my father's words were a vote of confidence in his young son or whether he thought this was an expense he had successfully avoided. My father was not the least bit embarrassed that he had just told his 13-year-old son that getting braces was completely dependent on his ability to produce $700 to cover one-third of the overall cost. My father was very, very tight with his money and may have even viewed braces as an unnecessary luxury. I am certain the orthodontist thought he would never see me in his office again and perhaps my father believed the same thing. However, they were both wrong.

At the time, minimum wage was only $1.60 an hour, and I was not even eligible to work. My father was not the least bit interested in hearing how challenging it would be for a 13-year-old boy to raise $700, nor did I attempt to share my view of that challenge with him.

I knew that raising my portion of the fee was my own problem and not my father's. End of the discussion. I left the orthodontist's office motivated as ever to get those braces, and I was not the least bit discouraged regarding the money I had to raise. The world didn't owe me a thing. Period.

It took me four months to raise the $700 required for me to finally get my braces. Thankfully during that same summer, the Chicago Board of Education offered jobs that were available to anyone 13 or older. I lucked out and landed a job cleaning up the exterior of public schools in some neighborhoods that were considered very rough at that time. It was the summer of 1972, and my salary was $2 an hour for the job that was to last for approximately eight weeks. I saved just about every dime I made and supplemented my income washing cars, cutting grass, and cleaning out garages for folks in the neighborhood.

I kept my savings in a White Owl cigar box, and when I had finally amassed the $700 needed to begin work on my teeth, I brought it downstairs and proudly handed it to my father.

He looked a bit surprised when I handed him that box, but the smile on his face was one of both amazement and pride. However, it would take many more years beyond this occasion before I would hear my father actually say the following words:

"I'm proud of you."

I can still remember exactly where and when he first spoke those words to me. I was 35 years old and visiting Chicago with my son, Matthew, who was only three years old at the time. I had taken my father and Matthew to a park situated near Lake Michigan. As we drove home after spending a few hours outside, we traveled past 53rd and Cottage Grove when my father said to me, "Boy, I am so proud of you." The words came out of nowhere. We were just riding along enjoying a beautiful day and time spent together. I had waited so long to hear those words, yet when I finally heard him utter those few words, I was speechless as tears welled in my eyes. He may not have actually spoken those words to me the moment I handed him that cigar box that contained my end of the infamous *Braces Agreement*, but the look on his face at that moment told me everything I needed to know.

First, I saw sheer amazement because I did not share any progress reports with my father. Then, I saw pride. My father was a man of his word, so I was back in the orthodontist's office to begin treatment the following week. I never asked my father why he made me raise $700 to begin the process of getting braces, nor if he intended a life's lesson through this transaction. I do believe that my father wanted to know I was committed to doing what I needed to do while wearing braces, and I suppose he felt that if I raised the necessary funds, I might be equally committed to caring for my braces once they were applied to my crooked teeth.

Obstacle to success? You bet it was, but it was not an insurmountable one.

Money was incredibly important to my father; I suspect he wanted to see my level of ownership of my objective of getting braces in the primary language he used to judge one's pledge or promise to almost anything: money.

These two brief stories, and others I will share throughout this book, serve as partial answers regarding my beliefs. The number of negative incidents I have been subjected to strike me as both extremely limited in number and utterly insignificant to my journey to adulthood and beyond. This book is in part an exploration of why the emotions conjured in me when confronted with racially-biased incidents have seemingly differed so significantly from those of so many of my friends and colleagues and why that mattered across my careers in the military, the FBI, and in the private sector. However, I hope by reading to the end, you will ultimately have an innovative approach for navigating the world in which we live today. There will always be bullies, sexists, racists, bigots, and other negative characters the world would be far better off without. It would be a far more peaceful world if our focus was on character, honesty, integrity, and a host of more appealing characteristics that have nothing to do with one's race or gender.

However, since a world free of such obstacles is unlikely to be inhabited by any of us anytime soon, I have always looked to myself to navigate unfriendly, unkind, and even hostile environments in which I have found myself. What I have never done is shrink from those environments and seek a safe harbor in which to nurse hurt feelings or a wounded psyche.

I embrace the idea that the world owes me nothing, and I have lived my life never wanting to be anyone's victim.

This concept led to my ability to brush off incidents that impacted others so strongly and so negatively. I know inequities exist. I know people whose professional lives have been impacted by unfairness, from hiring through promotions and, too often, right through to retirement. However, I want to focus on what each of us can do to prepare ourselves to be the best we can be and challenge this world and its inherent obstacles as gladiators and not mere spectators. You cannot stay down because someone else thinks you should. Although my father's words, *"Boy, this world owes you nothing,"* at times filled me with trepidation, I believe my embrace of those words has added a measure of steel to the hull of my life's ship.

Chapter Four

Let No One Hold Dominion Over You

"You better be careful walking around the back of this horse, because this horse hates niggers, and if he sees a nigger; he will kick his head off."

-Mendel Catholic High School Football Player

I have an inherent belief that we sometimes confuse our own desires with expectations to which we hold others accountable that they are under no obligation to meet. We may want to be included in a particular group, but some may be resistant to offering us full acceptance into that group. This may occur despite you having passed all the requisites of their *membership*. I have seen folks get passed over from a promotion for which they were clearly qualified. Unfortunately, some have allowed a single such snub change their attitude about pursuing other opportunities. I have had more than one mentee exclaim to me, "What's the point? I'll never get promoted, so why keep trying?"

Even as a young boy, I never let anyone deter me from pursuing a goal I'd set for myself. Perhaps I was terribly naïve about the realities of the world, leading me to actually believe I could pursue whatever goals I desired.

When I was a student at the FBI Academy, I had a class that required the students to write an incident report. I had a classmate who had been a state trooper prior to joining the FBI. Several students, including myself, sought his counsel for completing this particular exercise. I completed my report in the manner in which I'd been advised by this student and thought I'd done a fairly decent job. The instructor who graded my report clearly disagreed

45

with my assessment. The marks on the paper actually looked angry. What I remember most clearly about this particular episode is not the grade I received, but the comments the grader thought were appropriate for inclusion in his remarks.

He wrote, *"This is the worst report I have ever seen. I don't know how this individual ever qualified for an appointment as a Special Agent of the FBI!"*

Becoming an FBI Special Agent was literally a lifelong dream of mine. One might think such remarks would have broken my spirit, but his words did not have any impact on me at all. Yes, I did seek a bit of constructive criticism, none of which was to be found in any of the remarks on my paper. However, his remarks were so over-the-top, I was immediately dismissive of his opinion of my work. I almost laughed! I'd worked my ass off to get into the FBI. This was one small exercise in one class, and he was already judging my overall suitability to join the ranks that included him.

A tiny part of me wondered if my grader was aware of the composition of our class and was bothered by that fact. Ironically, my New Agents Class (NAC) was probably one of the most diverse in the FBI's history. Let me be both fair and completely transparent here. I have no knowledge of the gender or race of my grader, nor did I see any Black instructors during my time as a student at the Academy. My point is that I had no intention of surrendering my dream or my passion to achieve that dream to someone whose overly broad opinion of me was based on a single paper.

When I encounter someone with a broken spirit, it saddens me because I know each of us is our own best advocate. The story below will illustrate how the individual who graded my paper had no chance of deterring me or putting a chill on my motivation to continue forward. As you will see from the little vignette below, the individual who so harshly offered his opinion of my suitability to join the community of FBI agents had no chance of dissuading me from the pursuit of my lifelong ambition.

I attended high school at Mendel Catholic High on Chicago's Southside. Consistent with his philosophy that *the world owes me nothing*, my father agreed to pay for one-half of the tuition, and I covered everything else, to include books, lunches, bus fare, etc. One of the things the school's faculty constantly preached was the value of being a "Mendel Man," which encompassed being part of a community of boys who were expected to mature into productive men and contribute to the world in which we lived.

I liked the idea of belonging to something bigger than myself, the idea of being part of a larger community. As a result, becoming a Mendel Man meant something to me.

Early into my first semester of high school there was a beautiful black horse on campus. Although I had no idea why the horse was there, I had always loved horses, so I decided to go over and get a closer look. As I approached the horse, I noticed three white students were also looking at the thoroughbred. All were members of the school's football team whom I had admired from afar. One of the football players saw me and said,

"You better be careful walking around the backside of this horse..."

In that instant, I felt a surge of pride. I felt as though this big football player and upperclassman felt protective of me—a lowly, first-year student—and was looking out for my welfare. I thought this is what it was like to be a part of the Mendel Community. Well, those thoughts came crashing back down to earth when the next words out of his mouth were:

"...because this horse hates niggers, and if he sees a nigger, he will kick his head off."

Now, as a freshman in high school, I stood 5'7" tall and weighed about 105 lbs. soaking wet, so fighting was not an option, nor is it one I would have likely chosen if I had been larger than that offending student. One his friends laughed, and the other guy looked a little bit embarrassed, but said nothing in my defense. However, that statement did not hurt my feelings or even alter the attitude I carried for the rest of the day. Believe it or not, it did not even make me mad. I just thought:

That guy's an asshole.

I went back to class and honestly do not remember sharing that story with anyone as it was just a simple hiccup in an otherwise good day.

What's my point? The student who spoke those ugly words to me is someone I saw almost exclusively on the football field. We were not friends, and he had no influence on my life. He didn't even owe it to me to be kind. I would argue that as a fellow student and an upperclassman, he should have felt a responsibility to set a good example of what it meant to be a *Mendel Man*, but as you have just read, he failed miserably in that regard. Yes, I do remember the story with crystal clarity, but it has never evoked any feelings of anger in me. His statement was a racist epithet undoubtedly intended to hurt my feelings. He failed miserably in that regard as well. It is important to note that I simply did not care what his motivation was for mistreating me:

He hated freshmen; he especially hated black freshman, or he hated that the school was slowly, but clearly, moving from a white majority student base to one that was majority black.

All the probabilities were his problem. Might he have said similarly unkind words to another white student who happened to be fat, super-skinny, wore thick eyeglasses, or was otherwise viewed as an appropriate target for a stupid insult? Absolutely! The guy was a class-A asshole. Of course, I did not want to be mistreated or disrespected, but since I could not change the course of events that day, I just moved on without another care in the world. I even like to imagine that when that now former football player remembers this story—though I doubt that he has given it a second thought—he may regret what he said to me that day. Of course, he might also just be a 66-year-old asshole.

When I joined my first office after becoming an FBI Special Agent, I was warmly welcomed by the entire office, all of whom were white except for one. I remember feeling as though I had made the right decision by pursuing an appointment as an FBI Special Agent because that first office represented the kind of environment I was hoping to find in my new career. The agents seemed to really care about their work and the office exuded a professional atmosphere that I had hoped to find in my first office. Approximately three months later, another new (white) agent joined the office and was someone with whom I became good friends. One day as we were out pursuing a lead, he mentioned to me that he was looking forward to finally having a Friday free, without a dinner commitment. I asked him what he was talking about, and he told me that the guys in the office had all been inviting him to dinner at their homes. My first thought was,

Hmmm, no one has yet invited me to dinner at their home.

However, I breezed right past that thought because none of my colleagues owed me an invitation to their homes for dinner!

What they "owed" me was to treat me like a fellow agent, and as a new agent, it was incumbent upon them to teach me how to navigate through my first assignment. They all did that and much more. I accompanied just about every senior agent on multiple interviews, surveillances, and a host of other duties for which agents were responsible. I loved my *first-office* experience. I was eventually invited to the homes of most of the senior agents for dinner or backyard barbecues, which I really enjoyed.

The point of this story is that I refused to go around with my spirits shattered because I had not been invited to anyone's home in the four months preceding the arrival of my friend to our office. I did not withdraw from the company of my colleagues. I went for coffee and lunch with one or more of them practically every day. When I subsequently worked as an undercover agent on a number of narcotics investigations, those same colleagues protected me as if I were their brother, and that is something they *owed* me. While I

49

would have enjoyed being invited into the home of one or more of my colleagues for dinner early in my tenure in the office, that is not something they owed me. However, those invitations did eventually come my way.

We all have the right to invite whomever we choose into our personal spaces. It is not an obligation of most professions. Many of the men and women I have mentored across my professional life have been terribly wounded by similar recollections or real time events in their own careers, and I have taken those occasions to share my philosophy with them. I just want them to separate something they might desire from the things they are owed. Is it easy to compartmentalize your life? Of course not, but I would offer one thing to bolster my personal philosophy in this space.

I am a hopeless optimist and almost perpetually in a good mood. I think part of this stems from an ability to intellectually move past nonsense that ultimately has no bearing on my life.

More recently, a mentee contacted me about a meeting she had requested with human resources, the company's Equal Employment Opportunity Office (EEOO), and her immediate supervisor. She told me she called the meeting because she was tired of being treated in a manner she deemed completely inappropriate. The meeting was confirmed on the calendar, and now she was seeking advice on how she should use this meeting.

The first thing I asked her to do was describe exactly why she felt as though she was receiving second-class treatment compared with her colleagues.

She said her boss routinely met with the other engineers for coffee and lunch as a group, but she was never invited to join the group nor invited to share a cup of coffee with the boss.

My mentee went on to tell me that she was routinely interrupted during her presentations in a manner that belittled her efforts. She further stated that the boss often praised the other managers for the work of their teams, but despite equal or superior outcomes produced by her team, she never received public (or private) praise as her colleagues had many times over. She then told me her annual appraisal was supposedly based on definitive metrics of success, all of which she had achieved at a level meeting or exceeding her colleagues, yet her appraisal was tepid at best and her bonus was also less than that received by her colleagues.

It is relevant that she was both the only female in the group and the only black person.

My first piece of advice for my mentee to follow during her meeting was to not begin her presentation by telling everyone she was the only female and the only black person in the group. Why? First, it gives her boss an easy out. For instance, her boss will not likely say,

"You know, you're right. I never wanted a female in my group and don't particularly care for having a black person in my group, and that is why I have treated you as I have these past six months."

That statement has probably never been uttered by anyone in such a meeting and certainly not anyone who had hoped to continue working for the company. The obvious response is far more likely to begin with a denial that her race or gender had anything to do with any of her complaints. It is almost impossible to prove such a point anyway, and trying to do so just clouds the actual issues. One might think I do not believe race or gender matter. That is not true; however, I go back to my thoughts regarding what the world owes any of us. I do not care if someone does not like me because I am Black or because I am tall or for any other reason. I cannot fix what is in someone's heart, nor in many instances do I care to attempt to do so. I advised my mentee to focus on the tangible acts committed by her boss that were (and should have been) offensive to her, and to anyone else for that matter. I then challenged her to think about what she was solving for, i.e., what did she want to accomplish from the planned meeting? She said she simply wanted to be treated as a full-fledged member of the team and respected as a fellow engineer. She wanted her reviews to reflect her tangible metrics of success. *Why* someone is treating you inappropriately is far less relevant than the fact they *are* treating you unfairly.

Stop worrying about their motivations, because you can rarely prove what motivates someone, and suggesting you have been treated unfairly because of your race, gender, religion, or sexual orientation is typically nonproductive and often leaves the real issues without resolution.

If my neighbor was throwing rocks through the windows of my house, the first thing I would want to do is bring that activity to an immediate halt. The second thing I would want to do is ensure he paid for all the repairs caused by his actions. I do not care *why* he started throwing rocks through my windows. Think of it this way: is my neighbor likely to offer an explanation that would result in my saying,

"Okay, now I get it. Go ahead and keep throwing rocks through my windows"? Hell No!

My mentee's mistake was that she focused on her gender and race as the issue when obviously her boss was going to claim neither had anything to do with how he interacted with her. I advised her to make him answer the question regarding why she had been treated like a second-class citizen and to raise very specific actions which made her feel this way. The treatment she described to me would offend *anyone,* and his motivations are ultimately meaningless because his motivations will not justify his actions.

When I was working in the Washington D.C. office of the FBI—an office I would eventually lead as Assistant Director-in-Charge later in my career—I was working on a white-collar crime squad. We were working in a dump of an office in a less-than-desirable area of town but were slated to move into a new office in the near future. One day the boss invited us all to see the new office and to locate our new desk. There were 17 agents on the squad, but only 14 desks had been provided to our squad in the new office. Three of us did not have desks assigned, including me.

The one other Black special agent and one of the two females on the squad were among the excluded. The other two agents had more time on the squad (and in the FBI) than all but two of the 14 agents who had desks assigned. I was newer to the squad and to the FBI, but senior to at least four of the agents who received desk assignments.

As just about every little perk in the FBI is based on seniority, I could not help myself. I asked the agent responsible for assigning desks how he determined who was going to be assigned the initial group of desks assigned to our squad?

He responded to my gentle inquiry by saying, "Oh, here we go again with another EEO complaint!" Having never made such a complaint in my entire professional life, I just punted that comment away. I told him I was simply curious as to how the seating arrangements were made. Alphabetically, my last name and the other Black agent's last name fell into the middle of the alphabet. The three of us were all senior to at least a portion, if not all, of the agents who received desk assignments. I was the tallest guy on the squad! I wanted the person responsible for assigning the desks, regardless of his motivation or lack thereof, to see what he had done, i.e., failing to reserve a desk for two of the squad's most senior agents.

I know, I know, many will exclaim, "Oh my God! Are desk assignments that big of a deal?" Of course not, especially if YOU got a desk. It is a small thing, really. It was a small slight, but not an unimportant slight. How often are similarly small complaints dismissed by those who have never suffered such slights? However, it is less about the actual slight than the feelings it engenders of never really being part of the club and of always being on the outside looking in.

I was not angry or hurt about not having a desk assigned, but neither was I going to let the matter pass without a conversation aimed at educating my colleague. My point is that I stayed focused on what I was solving for.

I wanted the agent responsible for assigning desks to realize what he had done, and I was giving him the benefit of the doubt by not concluding that his heart was filled with malice. Why? Again, because I did not care what was in his heart. Using any of the common metrics the FBI commonly uses, all three of us should have been assigned desks in the new office while those junior to us waited for the shortage of desks in our area of the office to be addressed. However, my goal, as you will see in a later story, was to educate, not obliterate. The three of us were eventually assigned nice window seats, which were prime real-estate in the office desk wars.

What I cared about was being treated as a member of the team and not someone still trying to earn his spurs. It was important for me to speak up lest, assuming his heart was good, the results of his decision-making process go completely unnoticed.

Although we all need people who support, guide and mentor us, *you* are the most valuable asset you control. Our spirit, enthusiasm, motivation, focus, and drive are all ours to calibrate and engage as we deem appropriate. I would never let someone negatively impact any of those components of my life and neither should you. Focus on the tangible aspects of any professional problem you are trying to solve. Emotion is like the fat in a really good steak. A little bit adds flavor, but too much renders the meat unsatisfactory. I could have started the conversation accusing the person responsible for assigning seats that he missed me and my other two colleagues because one, like me, was black and the other a female. However, I did not care about the *why*, only the outcome.

I have seen far too many legitimate complaints go up in smoke and remain unresolved because the conversation turned to the offender's motivations rather than his or her behavior. It is always the latter that matters most.

I genuinely believe that a lot of valuable time is wasted trying to determine why we have been treated in a particular manner when what really matters is stopping the offensive behavior.

Chapter Five

No Excuses

"Man, if I ever learned someone I was working with was working with the police, that's the first motherfucker I'd kill if I was being arrested."

-Criminal informant I would soon arrest

The mentors I have introduced you to thus far were influencers in my life, and each shared a common characteristic to which I believe I was drawn. All of them saw at least one aspect of my relationship with them as clearly defined. They were people older than me by far and each felt they had something valuable to contribute to my maturation process. Whether they employed, taught, or coached me, they set expectations for me and fully expected that I would meet those expectations. Initially, I viewed many of their demands as beyond my current capabilities. However, these wonderful individuals were teaching me to reach farther than my own vision and challenge myself to be more. Dating back to when I played little league baseball, I encountered men who had simple demands and allowed few excuses for failure. My father was fond of saying:

"It doesn't matter whether your teacher loves you or hates you, 2+2=4, so I don't want to ever hear you make an excuse that you got a bad grade because your teacher doesn't like you."

As a result, I never sought such safe harbors for poor performances. I was expected to deal with the world as it existed and withstand its consequences for failure.

My first little league coach was Mr. Powell. He had no formal coaching experience but loved the game of baseball, and when he gave a player instructions, he expected that player to follow those instructions. The summer after I turned 12 years old, I played in my last season of little league games. I was pitching, and should make it clear right here that I was never particularly a gifted pitcher. Okay, I was never a particularly gifted *player* at any position, but I had heart and was about as earnest a player as there was on the field. During the middle of the game, a very powerful batter named Mark Scarborough was next to bat.

Mr. Powell was clear in his instructions to me: throw four balls and intentionally walk this batter.

I threw the first two pitches as instructed. Then, I saw a girl, Cheryl Johnson, who I spent my entire childhood chasing, sitting on the spectator bench. Well, there was no way she was going to see me intentionally walk this guy! I wound up and threw the baseball as hard as I could right down the middle of the plate. I recall whipping my head around and watching the beautiful trajectory of a ball hit squarely with the fat barrel of the bat. It took a path right out of Euclid Park and into the bushes of a house abutting the park. I also recollected that the right fielder never found that ball before being waved off by the umpire, lest the play of the game continue to be unnecessarily delayed.

Naturally, I also remember Mr. Powell pulling me out of the game and telling me to go and sit on the bench—the end of the bench. He never said another word to me that day despite my wanting him to royally chew me out for ignoring his instructions.

I knew he was disappointed in me and that bothered me more than any amount of yelling he might have levied upon me. I believe Mr. Powell saw the expression on my face and knew that I was sorry I had ignored his very clear instructions. I was even more sorry that the outfielder eventually took so much time looking for that ball, as his temporary absence from right field only drew more unwanted attention to that fateful pitch and my failure to follow Mr. Powell's instructions. The unfortunate outcome required the use of a new game ball, which was undoubtedly paid for by our coaches. We lost that game, but Mr. Powell never said anything else to me about the incident. He must have figured I'd learned a very valuable lesson. Specifically, when a powerful batter is facing a sub-par pitcher, there are exactly two options: walk him or get a new ball ready.

At another game, I played the position of catcher. I had gotten into a brief scuffle with the batter, Ray Adams. The umpire stepped in and told us both to knock it off and play ball. He followed with a stern warning, "If I hear another word from either of you, I will toss you out of the game." I retrieved my catcher's mask and assumed my position behind the plate. However, I just couldn't let it go. As I assumed my position behind the plate, I uttered something under my breath on the way down. I do not even remember what I said, but I recall with absolute clarity what occurred immediately after I'd uttered those words. The umpire looked at poor Mr. Powell and said, "Your catcher is ejected from this game."

And that was it. No appeal, no pleas for leniency or forgiveness. No apologizing. I'd been given a chance, and I tossed it to the winds. I was out of the game: period. I wasn't hurt or wounded. I'd tested the system and lost as the system fired right back at me. It was my fault—end of story.

One more story to make a point about decisions and accountability. When I was a freshman in high school, my English teacher, Mr. Mike Curtin, called me up to receive my first-quarter semester grade. Mr. Curtin had a piece of paper on his desk. It had a large A, B, and C written on it. He pointed to the C and said, "I could sleep well if I gave you that grade, because that is most accurately the grade you have earned." He then pointed at the B and said, "But that is the grade I am giving you because it's a very close call." However, it is what he said next that puts him in the bucket of influencers in my life who made a definitive difference in the path I chose. Mr. Curtin went onto say,

"You are capable of getting this grade (pointing at the A). Don't be a clown like some of the students in this class. You know better and are capable of more. Now go and sit down."

Done. No excuses and no explanations wanted or needed. Just go and sit down. I did earn three A's in the following three quarters, but I am almost certain, save for Mr. Curtin's words, I would not have done so on my own. I feasted on high expectations and whenever presented with an elevated level of expected performance, I just naturally tried to achieve or surpass those expectations.

I also believe I felt a strong need to be liked, which has not always served me well across my professional life and a point I will address later.

While these stories occurred relatively early in my life, I believe all significantly contributed to the man I was to later become. I was given no opportunity to feel sorry for myself, and in the moment following each of the aforementioned stories, I had time to sit down and embrace my responsibility for the outcome of each of those scenarios. In my adult life, I have always focused on my performance, my preparation, and my execution. If I failed to receive a desired rating, performance mark, rank, or position that I felt I was well positioned to receive, my immediate response was always to first examine myself and my contribution to the situation confronting me. I have long felt it is simply too easy to constantly view every failure we experience as the result of an external attribute we cannot control, to include racism.

I am not naïve and realize that racism and sexism have been responsible for the denial of opportunities for millions of people since the dawn of time and continue to cloud judgements regarding the chosen recipients of one benefit or another.

However, you cannot change anyone's heart. You cannot make them accept what their inherent biases will not allow them to accept, so you have focus on the one thing you control—you. Universities, companies, government agencies and each of us as individuals, have a responsibility to combat racial, gender, age, and sexual orientation discrimination. All must work to eliminate the impact any of those characteristics within the workplace. Those battles must continue until every vestige of their negative impact has been eliminated. That is, of course, a very long-range view and none of us can wait until the perfect balance of diversity, equity, and inclusion has been reached.

Ultimately, I do not care about how people feel or think per se. I care how and when their inappropriate thoughts or attitudes negatively impact decisions that should be made based on performance or attributes that do not include one's race, gender or sexual preferences.

Nevertheless, I continue to believe it is self-defeating to immediately retreat to the safe harbor of discrimination as the reason we did not receive whatever form of recognition we feel we were due. Doing so relieves us of the need to conduct any critical examination of our own performance, not to mention other contributing factors which could have contributed to our failures. You allow yourself to move forward on the presumption that you are already the best you can possibly be and clearly better than your competition. Your educational background, experience and interview were clearly devoid of any shortcomings. There is no need for any critical performance review, nor is there anything else that might have impacted the situation, other than your rationale for your failure.

My other problem with assuming racism or sexism played a role in your non-selection for a job or promotion is that it doesn't require any examination of your competition.

Racism and sexism have served as negative determinants in recruiting, hiring, training and promotions for centuries—no debate there at all. People have been, and are present day, excluded from consideration for hire and promotions based on a wide array of irrelevant considerations. Most of us can easily point to plenty of clear-cut examples in which someone was denied a job, an assignment, or advancement based on the biases of those making the selections. I have never seen the value in focusing on something that, *in the moment,* I cannot change. Rather, if the decision is to be challenged, one's portfolio of work must be able to withstand critical examination. I want to control that which I can control.

I must admit at this point in the book that I have never felt as though I did not receive something because of the inherent racism in either the process or in individuals responsible for making such decisions. I know how lucky I am to be able to write such a statement, but that is my reality, and I will not alter that reality to somehow make this book appear to be more authentic.

I must also admit that I was not selected for only one position I applied for during the entirety of my FBI career. In that instance, I also happened to believe the individual selected (white female) was more qualified than me because she was already "inspection-certified," which made one's bid for a supervisory position in the FBI a bit more compelling. Some might argue that my experience is a poor platform from which to offer the lessons I have raised thus far, but I do not share that opinion. Let me make it clear that the message of this book is categorically not, "If I did it, why can't you?" My intention is to discuss what I view as failed strategies and meaningless responses to failures beyond one's control. If there is one thing that I fervently believe, it is that I am responsible for my own attitude and for the decisions I make every single day of the year. *I own me.* The following story illustrates someone who clearly shared a similar philosophy.

I have been the villain in at least one situation in which my actions negatively impacted someone else. I was a 27-year-old FBI Special Agent working in an undercover capacity. The following incident occurred when it was time to bring an investigation, in which I was the undercover agent, to a close. The conclusion of the case involved the arrest of the subject, and it was planned to occur a few days after the following exchange: I was briefing my fellow FBI agents and our partners in the state and local police regarding the plans for the arrest of this particular subject. The meeting took place in a conference room inside our FBI office; however, there were not sufficient chairs for all the members of the task force to be seated, so I went into the outer office looking for additional chairs. I saw a vacant chair next to the desk of one of my colleagues, Carol Philip-Sydnor. She was a Black female and one of only three Black agents in that division at the time. Moreover, Carol and I were the only Black agents in the satellite office where this case was being worked, with the third Black agent assigned to our headquarters city office in New Haven, Connecticut.

I approached Carol's desk, then reached out and grabbed the chair next to her desk while I simultaneously explained that I needed to borrow it for the meeting I was hosting. Carol then reached out, pulled her chair back, and told me that I could not borrow her chair. She was smiling, so I initially assumed she was joking. She was not. Carol said:

"This is the third or fourth case in which you have been the undercover and have been responsible for planning the take down of the case. You have never asked me to join the arresting team even once. I was a Baltimore cop for six years before joining the FBI. I worked in some of the roughest neighborhoods in Baltimore during my time serving with the police department. I suspect I have more hands-on arrests than most of the state troopers, many of the young police officers back there, and almost certainly all of the agents on the team. Yet, you have never sought my assistance or asked me to join the team. If you can't use me, you can't use my chair."

Carol was smiling, but she was dead serious. I let go of her chair. I then told Carol that I wanted to use her chair and that she should sit in it and join the team. The story did not end with that simple resolution, not by a long shot. Carol was right on target. I had denied her the opportunity to participate in work through which FBI agents and others in law enforcement earn a great deal of credibility. Everything Carol said to me during our exchange was information I was already very much aware of, and she was right. I'd never asked Carol to assist us on any prior arrest. I asked myself for months after this conversation occurred how I could have ignored her in such a manner, especially since the two of us represented two-thirds of the Black Special Agents assigned to the entire New Haven field office at that time.

The fact of the matter is that I never consciously or intentionally excluded Carol. Not once had I ever thought to myself or said aloud to others, "I'll never use a female on arrest scenarios in which I am the undercover." The hard truth is that none of that matters, nor am I looking to make a convenient excuse for myself. The motivation or lack of motivation for excluding Carol is secondary to what I had actually done and, sadly, done multiple times. I excluded her, and she had nailed me right between the running lights. I did not have, nor did I want any place to hide. I engaged in a lot of introspection in the wake of this incident and vowed to myself never to be guilty of such blatantly biased conduct ever again in my professional life.

There are multiple lessons to be derived from this story, and it is one that I have shared with dozens of audiences. In one such presentation, I was asked by a female member of the audience a very simple question: "Why did you exclude Carol from such operations?"

It was a perfectly legitimate question and one I was hoping to be asked. As I wrote earlier, I never consciously excluded Carol. She was, and still remains, my dear friend! This incident was far more than a minor speedbump in a career filled with more minor speedbumps; this was by far one of the most meaningful moments of my FBI career. That single exchange played as great a role as anything in my experience to that point in my career in shaping the type of leader I was to become. It literally impacted the remainder of my professional career in the FBI and far beyond. It doesn't matter what's in your heart or head. What ultimately matters is what you *actually do* and the impact of those actions. If I had been asked for my opinion of female law enforcement agents, I would have given the most open-minded and inclusive response possible. I had done so on a number of occasions prior to this incident. However, that is not the person I was to Carol.

The first lesson to be learned is:

This incident showed me the importance of constantly evaluating yourself to ensure that you align with the person you think you are. This is even more vital if you are in a leadership role as your decisions can have many unintended consequences.

I had never subjected myself to any type of introspective examination of who I thought I was at that time. I'd never questioned my decisions nor reviewed my decisions to uncover hidden biases while in the FBI or in my prior time as an officer in the U.S. Marine Corps. To this day, I am so grateful this situation occurred when I was 27 and not much older. This incident made me very conscious of ensuring that in all future personnel decisions, I intentionally considered the entire universe of talented individuals for whatever matter was present before me. This story played a significant role in shaping the leader I was to become in the FBI. So, it is critical that we all periodically pause and take stock of ourselves. It should be a time to ask ourselves hard questions about who we think we are, not just in the eyes of other people, but in our own accounting of ourselves. When you are in a position of authority, such introspection is even more critical.

Are you really open-minded and focused on the entire universe of the people who work for you? Have you considered employees who you do not see every day? Are you using legitimate metrics to determine the relative success of those you supervise?

As someone competing for a promotion, you could do a complete examination of all the facts and a self-analysis of your performance and still question why you were not promoted, selected for a special assignment, or accorded some other form of beneficial treatment. Then it becomes a question of how you handle that conclusion. You need to examine your options carefully, but remaining silent should not be on your list. I mentioned earlier that I was only passed over for one position I had applied for in my FBI career. Intellectually, I of course realized that I might not be the selected candidate for the position as others in the package may have been more competitive. In my opinion, that is exactly what happened when I was passed over for the first supervisor position I pursued. As it happens, in this instance, I was told by a participant on the career board that the individual responsible for advocating for me on the career board remained silent throughout the discussion of candidates for this position.

If the individual responsible for making the pitch for you remains silent, your candidacy for the position is dead-on-arrival. So, how did I handle that situation?

First, I knew I could not give up the source of my information because career board matters are conducted in private to allow all present to speak openly about each candidate for the position being discussed. However, I decided to approach my Assistant Director (AD) and make one simple request: If the division was not going to support my candidacy, I requested to be advised of their position and presented with an opportunity to discuss what they might have viewed as my shortcomings for the position. I did not accuse anyone of failing to advocate for me nor make any other allegations that I could not prove just because I was a bit upset.

Rather, I presented a request to the AD that I felt confident was going to cause him to have a conversation with our division's career board representative regarding that specific career board, i.e., "What happened in yesterday's career board regarding Mason's application?"

That is precisely what occurred. I subsequently had a conversation with the division's career board representative, and rather than attack his failure to properly represent me (which would have required me giving up my source of information), I merely advised that if the division felt I was unqualified for a position, I would rather know that prior to the career board meeting. I made my request appear to be something I wanted to be sure of prior to putting in additional applications for future supervisory vacancies. Such knowledge would have allowed me to make my case for why I believed I was well qualified for the position, or if after a good discussion I felt otherwise, I could reconsider and possibly withdraw my application. Despite the fact that I felt the eventual recipient of the position was more qualified for the position than me, I still felt as though our representative had an obligation to earnestly represent the personnel from our division, obviously including me, and that did not happen in my case.

When speaking to power, you must always know what you are solving for, otherwise the conversation can go off the rails in seconds.

I was seeking to ensure I would either be told the division was not going to support my candidacy for a position or to be well represented when the board focused on a vacancy I was hoping to fill. It was not necessary, nor would I have ever betrayed the confidence my source had placed in me by telling me I was poorly represented in the questioned career board.

The second lesson to be learned from this story is:

One must have complete ownership of their own career (not *control* as that is not always possible). Absent the courage of Carol to refuse to continue to be treated like a second-class special agent, this scenario might have played out many more times during our shared time together in that particular office.

I never once considered the fact that I had not asked Carol to join us. I can write very honestly that I never *intended* to disrespect Carol, but none of that really matters. What matters is what I did. Remember my earlier discussion of desires versus legitimate expectations?

Carol had every legitimate expectation to be included in all manner of the office's operations, high risk or otherwise. She wasn't seeking to be my friend or have me include her when I went out for coffee. Carol was expecting to be treated like every other agent and that was not happening. So, it was time for Carol to decide. There are always risks when someone decides to take a stand, and it is not my intention here to pretend such risks don't exist. What follows is something many will want to instinctively argue against, but I ask your indulgence to finish reading this portion of the book and take the time to consider what I have written.

The risks for Carol, while none were career-ending, could have affected the remainder of her time in that particular office.

I could have told her, "I'll find more chairs somewhere else, keep your damn chair." I could have then shared the story with my colleagues, filled with my version of the facts and turned the office against Carol. The vast majority of the other agents in the office had prior military experience as I did, and equally importantly, most were men. We were in the middle of an important event, and I could have made Carol look petulant or somehow immature when she was neither. I could have complained to our boss, who I am sure would have sided with me and told Carol to give me the chair. After all, we had outside colleagues in the office and this was no time to be quibbling over the use of a chair.

However, in reality, this had nothing to do with a chair but everything to do with my colleague being treated as an equal to every other agent in the office. If she didn't address this situation, who was going to do it on her behalf? Let me assure you, the answer to that question at that time was, "No one." Carol had options. She could have decided to not say anything and simply waited until she was transferred to another office (as all first-office agents eventually were at that time). She also could have just faded into the woodwork, assumed making arrests was the work of the men in the office, or just decided staying quiet was the path of least disruption and *better for her career.* Carol was "guilty" of being right and in that moment, she decided that she had endured enough.

Carol chose to take a stand for herself. She wasn't going to wait for fate to intervene or for an enlightened boss to recognize that she had not been included in high risks scenarios by a fellow agent.

She had waited long enough, and the time to act was upon her. Despite the fact that both Carol and I were fairly new agents, I still consider her response to being excluded from my investigations as a very courageous act. Carol spoke to me in a very level tone of voice. She smiled throughout the exchange and spoke with very little emotion.

She wasn't angry, but neither was she going to back down. She was direct and supported by facts which she laid out very clearly. Again, Carol was "guilty" of being right.

I have no doubt that Carol handled later situations immediately without allowing the transgressor time to see his or her error in thinking. I wasted the opportunities Carol gave me to see the error of my ways. Again, I may have never seen my mistakes if Carol had not confronted me with such an obvious and clear act of exclusion.

Perhaps the third and most important lesson to be taken from this story is:

Avoid automatically assuming the worst in people due to discriminatory labels we so quickly and generously apply often times without sufficient evidence.

Until the end of my time on earth, I will stand by my statement that I never intentionally excluded Carol. During all the takedown operations I had previously planned, she had somehow become invisible to me. Obscure to another Black person who considered her to be my friend—and thankfully, we are dear friends to this day. Invisible to one of only three Black agents in the entire division. There was never any malice aforethought and never a hidden agenda that would lead me to *not* include Carol or any other female agent in such operations. However, that is exactly what I did.

The consequences of our acts are not dependent solely on our motivations. Whether I intended to exclude Carol is irrelevant to the fact that *I did exclude Carol.* The opportunity for her to earn credibility among the mostly male office was lost as a result of my unconscious bias. This story ends with Carol being assigned as my side-by-side partner in subsequent undercover investigations. She was not merely part of the arrest team; she was my *partner*. She sat beside me during a number of dangerous scenarios, and she evolved to become the person I counted on to help keep us both safe.

Carol was far from being invited into the tail-end of a case; I also made her my partner at critical junctures of subsequent investigations. One of those cases is worth sharing to best illustrate the value of talent that is too often untapped. I was working on an investigation which was due to conclude in a few days with the arrest of the subject. I had been working this case for a couple of months and bought various quantities of cocaine from him. When we met for the first time, I remember he told me:

"Man, if I ever learned someone I was working with was working with the police, that's the first motherfucker I'd kill if I was being arrested."

Make a mental bookmark of that statement as it will matter later in this story. As soon as it spit from his lips, I immediately locked it in my head, which made each of the following transactions a bit more tense. On the day of the arrest of this subject, after a 2-3 month undercover investigation, Carol accompanied me and took on the role of my girlfriend. Together, we drove to the site at which the exchange of money for cocaine was to occur. I had arranged with the subject to meet at one location, and I would then follow him to a second location to complete the deal. Half of the arrest team followed me to the first location and the other half of the team proceeded to what was supposed to be the take-down location.

Code words were given if the scenario changed and the arrest needed to be executed at the first meeting location. I told the arrest team the following, "If I give the signal to execute the arrest, just approach his car in a normal manner, i.e., no lights and sirens, no driving where cars don't belong so as not to alert him to your presence prematurely." Well, as it often happens, a few folks must have been daydreaming when I gave those instructions, because when I gave the code words to execute the arrest, cars came flying from everywhere including across a park adjacent to the street on which the subject was sitting. I was parked next to the curb, with a car in front of me and behind me and his car was parallel to my car and in the traffic lane. He immediately recognized that he was about to start a very bad day and attempted to reach in between the front driver and passenger seats.

Once I gave word to execute the arrest, I reached for my gun that I had placed beneath my seat. However, I could not reach it as it had slid into the rear passenger compartment!

I thought the subject was reaching for a gun and already knew what he had sworn he would do if he thought he was about to be arrested. I had nothing and simply pointed my finger at him and literally screamed, "Freeze!" Amazingly, he did freeze. In that precise moment I thought, "I still have that commanding Marine Corps voice, which made him freeze when I only had a finger pointed at him." However, the truth of the matter is what I saw moments later after my tunnel vision, focused on his hand, returned to the normal 180 degrees. Carol had her gun pointed at the subject from the second I told him to freeze and that is why he stopped moving. It's worth sharing two final thoughts regarding this incident:

1. Carol's split-second decision to pull her gun likely prevented a bad outcome from a very high-stress incident. The person I had excluded from arrest scenarios proved to be the hero of the moment on that day.

2. I wondered for years afterwards if I had actually had my gun in my hand whether or not I would have shot the subject when his hand disappeared between the seats as I legitimately thought he was reaching for a gun (and remembered his promise to me on our initial visit). I could not see his hand. Had that situation advanced, I would have had less than a second to determine whether he actually

69

held a gun in his hand and then pray I would be faster than him.

He did not have a gun, only a balky brake release handle he could not get to move. Finally, and for the sake of a bit of humor, I realized right then and there that the male ego is astounding at times. I actually thought precisely what I wrote above: it was my voice that made him freeze!

Later, I laughed at myself! I have shared this story many times, and it is the women in the audience who love and are most engaged with that part of the story.

That day is now long gone, and I have worked to ensure every promotion, special assignment, or any other benefit that I controlled was fairly and transparently distributed. I have been privileged in both the FBI and in the private sector to hold senior executive positions. So, in addition to ensuring that I was fair and equitable in all of the promotions or special assignments I directly impacted, I have also worked purposefully to ensure that my staff did likewise. I believe that introspection is something everyone must possess, a real ability to examine oneself to ensure the manner in which you view yourself is the person you consistently present to the outside world.

While I believe racism and sexism continue to impact the advancement of many people of color and women, it is simply too easy to point to those as the constants in every decision regarding an advancement opportunity that involves majority and minority candidates.

Few hiring or promoting decisions are resolved early in the process and then narrowed down to just one or two candidates. I have mentored many people who have been quick to point to racism or sexism as the reason they were not selected despite the fact that the applicant pool included ten other highly qualified candidates. So, what reason can the other nine employees who were not selected point to for their failure to be selected? Might they all graciously assume they were less qualified than the person selected? I doubt it. My point is, the only avenue to success that I considered when applying for jobs or promotions was to make myself the most competitive candidate I could possibly be.

That lever is the only one I actually control. Is it possible that I might have been passed over just because I am a Black man? Absolutely. However, I cannot control that element. The only thing I can control is my ability to be the best prepared candidate I can be.

The need to make hiring, training, retention, and promotion processes fair and transparent must be an ongoing effort, and in many businesses and public agencies, it is. However, it is far from over and will continue for the lifetime of your author and, in all likelihood, the lifetimes of everyone who reads this book.

So, what do we do in the meantime? First, we must be willing to be our own best advocate. Complaining to friends and colleagues over lunch might prove to be a cathartic experience, but it is a poor substitute for raising your issue before those who are either part of it or can help to resolve it. Next, we have to be willing to step out of our comfort zone and speak to power. We have to be prepared with facts, not emotion, but raw facts. Most importantly, we have to realize that remaining silent *is a decision*. It is not what you are left with, but rather a conscious decision. I am not suggesting for a moment that potential real-life consequences don't matter. I am saying that only you can determine to what extent those real-life consequences, if they become a reality, may impact you and how you will respond to a particular set of circumstances.

Do you fear for your job? Do you fear you might be viewed as something other than a team player? Do you fear you might be passed over for a much sought-after promotion? These are all real-life possibilities, but throughout my professional life, I have owned every decision I have ever made, and fading away was never on my short list of possible options.

71

You don't get my sympathy for not speaking to power for fear of a possible negative outcome, but I am not without empathy because I understand possible outcomes that concern people who work for small-minded, vengeful superiors.

Nonetheless, I believe it is imperative to understand you are making a decision. If you choose not to act, then you must find a way to make your current circumstance work for you. Coming to work every day only to be miserable will eventually affect your performance, which in turn, and most ironically, will likely affect the upward path of your career. You have to embrace and live with the decisions you make. Perhaps the timing is not right, and you will pick up your lance and make your charge later.

Whenever someone tells me a story about how they have been or are currently being treated by an unfair boss, my very first question is, "What are you doing about it?" The conversation has no other place to begin.

I prefer not to wait to be invited to the table. I worked hard to put myself in positions in which I could be an active participant in hiring and promotion processes. I have relocated over ten times across my professional life and did so because it was necessary to continue to advance. I knew that I not only wanted to impact the trajectory of my professional life, but I wanted to be able to do so for others as well. The professional life I have enjoyed has been, in part, because I have stood on the shoulders of many who came before me. If you are the recipient of grossly unfair treatment in any of the spaces you occupy, there are multiple paths to resolution, including inaction, which rarely leads to the resolution of anything.

Your job is to select a course of action, and remaining silent or angrily complaining day after day over lunch to your friends and colleagues—and we all know such people—is not among the most effective paths you have to choose from to find real resolution. Anger is a useless emotion unless it drives you to resolution. Anger without action is surrender.

I have never spent much time considering the consequences of my addressing any workplace concern I experienced. I refused to make excuses that relieved me of any direct accountability for an undesirable outcome because I knew I must first review my own actions and preparations made pursuing my objectives. I wanted to know I had done all I could do to prepare myself. There may be legitimate reasons we failed to achieve one goal or another, but I believe an examination of the cause of any failure must necessarily begin internally by taking a hard look at ourselves first.

Chapter Six

Blinding Assumptions

"We all owe those who follow our paths to act as a source of light and enlightenment. The same struggles, obstacles, and landmines that challenge their journeys were once our own."

-Michael Mason

My lifelong goal in seeking the equitable treatment of myself and others has been to educate, not obliterate, people who strongly cling to poorly supported assumptions. I seek to do this regardless of who the victim of the perceived unjust treatment might be. I never want to jump on a bandwagon constructed of unfounded assumptions. I have had friends, colleagues and employees come to me with claims of having been treated unfairly in a hiring or promotion decision. Typically, they have been categorically certain that their treatment was the result of the biases of those making the selections. Such assumptions can lead to an endless cycle of failures if the conversation does end there. They might have been correct, but far too often they wanted the conversation to begin and end there. If the conversation ends there, what becomes of the possibility of learning something from that failure. Let me add that failure to be selected for a promotion should not necessarily be viewed as a failure in the usual sense of the word.

If I ran a race, but failed to finish first, have I actually failed? The answer to that question is dependent on how one defines failure.

I might have trained really hard, sacrificed good times to focus on my technique, rose early every morning confident I was preparing to be the very best I could be. However, on the day of the race, someone else was just a shade faster than me. Did I fail? In every competition in which I participated, my goal was to play the very best I could play. The outcome was important to me, but was not something I unilaterally controlled. So, if I left the field of play really knowing I had given all I had to give, but still lost, I did not leave despondent. I left knowing I had done my best. Hiring and promotion decisions are often made as a result of ever so slight differences in the appeal of one candidate over another. If you engage in an interview for a job, there are at least two things to be gained. First, you might get the job! Even if you fail to get the job, if you're a thinking person, you will emerge a bit wiser for your efforts. If the conversation ends with an embrace of a false rationale for being passed over, there will be no examination of a dozen other potential reasons you might not have been selected. One cannot change their race nor, for the sole purpose of getting a job, their gender, but what about our interviewing skills, the creativity of our responses, the depth of our responses, or our knowledge of the role we are seeking?

The following account represents a time when I had an opportunity to educate an employee who assumed a hiring decision was made based solely on the ethnicity of one of the applicants versus their qualifications. The "victim" of this apparent slight was not the employee herself, but her husband who had applied for a position in the office where she worked.

When I worked in the FBI's Inspection Division, I had the opportunity as an Assistant Inspector to work on an inspection of an FBI field office located in the midwestern portion of the country. Assistant Inspectors were often given additional duties during an inspection, and I was assigned to investigate an EEO complaint. I did my homework, properly researching all the relevant facts prior to meeting with the complainant, who was a white female FBI employee. I met with her close to one week after the team arrived onsite to conduct an inspection of the office's overall operations. The employee's complaint was fairly straightforward:

She believed her husband was not offered the position of 3rd Party Draft Officer because the office felt it needed to diversify its staff. A Black woman, whom she assumed held fewer qualifications, was selected to fill the vacancy.

This position was the equivalent of an entry-level bookkeeping position in which the incumbent was responsible for managing a wide variety of relatively small financial transactions required to keep the office running smoothly. The employee advised me that she was absolutely certain her husband was the superior candidate for the position, and from her vantage point, there is no way the selected applicant could possibly outperform her husband. I offer the last observation because I wondered whether she would have brought the complaint forward had a white man or woman been selected. This question arose in my mind because of what followed during the interview I conducted with the complainant.

The first issue I addressed with the complainant was her rationale for believing her husband was the superior candidate for the position, or at a minimum, more qualified than the Black female who was ultimately offered the position. I inquired whether her husband was a college graduate, and she replied that he had attended junior college but did not possess a four-year college degree. I asked about her husband's current position and learned he was a telephone lineman. I then asked what kind of relevant experience his background included that warranted her feelings that he was clearly the most competitive candidate for the position of 3rd Party Draft Officer?

She said that her husband was the bookkeeper for their church. I asked about the size of the church and she told me there were approximately 100 members of the congregation. I then asked what her husband's specific duties were in this role. She explained that he accounted for all contributions made to the church, paid the utility bills and handled small purchases on behalf of the ministry. In response, I stated that her husband's experience with their church certainly would have made him a competitive candidate for the position described above, and she readily agreed with my assessment.

I then asked the employee how much she knew about the background of the woman (I'll call her Debra) who was chosen to fill the position. She said that she knew nothing about Debra and had not even met her as she was a new employee and had only been with the office for a short period of time prior to the beginning of the inspection.

However, she admitted to knowing that the selected candidate was black, and, in the moment, that was the most important piece of information she apparently needed to arrive at the conclusion her husband had been unfairly denied the position.

As was previously stated, she was certain her husband's qualifications exceeded those of Debra. I then asked the complainant if she knew Debra was a college graduate who had earned a four-year degree in accounting? She responded, "No, I did not know that." I asked if she knew that Debra had an advanced degree in tax accounting and was also a Certified Public Accountant (CPA)? She responded, "No I did not know that either." I then asked the complainant whether she knew that Debra had formerly been the Chief Financial Officer for a midsized company and that she left that position a couple of years earlier to start a family. Again, the employee's response was the same.

I revealed to the complainant that Debra pursued the FBI job because it offered regular hours with weekends off—both of which accommodated Debra's new family lifestyle. It should be obvious by now that the complainant was oblivious to all of the facts I shared with her.

It is worthy of note that I did not present these facts in a mean, loud or nasty manner. I might as well have been giving her instructions on baking a cake. I was calm because I saw this not as an opportunity to shame anyone, but rather an opportunity to educate. At this point in our conversation, I could see that the complainant was starting to cry. I offered her some tissues, and she asked if she could be excused. Although I wanted the opportunity to wrap-up our conversation and seize the opportunity to make a few more points, I could see there was no value in proceeding with our interview at that time.

The conclusion to this story is just as important as the details that preceded it. Near the end of the same day that I interviewed the employee, she visited the work area where all the inspectors were assigned desks. There were numerous inspectors standing around talking when she appeared. She approached me and asked if she could give me a hug to which I responded, "Sure." She hugged me, and I asked her why she requested the embrace, though I was pretty certain of where we were going. At that point, she asked if we could speak privately. I located an interview room, and we both sat down to begin our second conversation of the same day.

She explained that I made her feel ashamed of herself, not because of how I handled the interview, but because I had confronted her with an aspect of herself she had never examined. The complainant had never viewed herself as anything other than a fair, unbiased person, and she realized the reality was something quite different.

She now realized that the views we hold of ourselves are often safe until the moment those views are challenged. She was ashamed of how she had clung to her belief that Debra was hired instead of her husband simply to satisfy what she believed was the office's desire to diversify its staff. The complainant told me that our conversation inspired her to confront an ugly truth about herself, but at the same time, she hoped that it made her wiser and more opened minded. She then acknowledged that Debra's qualifications for the position were indeed far superior to those of her husband's. She ultimately thanked me for opening her mind and more importantly, opening her heart. Mission accomplished.

When we assume a position based solely on our perceptions of the situation or the people involved, we can find ourselves embracing a conclusion unsupported by facts.

Had the employee at the center of the inspection story never raised her complaint, she might have gone through the immediate days, weeks, and months ahead with a bitter spirit and anger each time she encountered Debra. I hope she shared our exchange with others so that the lessons learned in our brief encounter would have an exponential and long-term effect on others. I would not want anyone to assume that there wasn't a measure of growth in the overall scenario for me. While I had done my homework and determined that Debra was the superior candidate for the job, which is why she was hired, I had to release any anger I felt at the complainant's incorrect supposition. This presented me with a small challenge because I quickly realized her supposition was based on a single factor: the race of the selected candidate.

I knew I needed to be armed with hard facts because when the complainant first met me, I suspected that she lost a bit of hope for her desired outcome because I, too, was black. She likely assumed that what she deemed an unfair, biased hiring decision would not be reversed nor would those responsible for this action be held accountable.

The complainant assumed that she was being bold in speaking to a truth she held in her heart, but which was clearly not supported by any factual information. I suspect this happens far more than most people are willing to acknowledge. I know I have often heard complaints where the offended individual had attached themself to a faulty set of assumptions, being either too lazy or too confident to believe there existed any other reasons for an outcome they have adjudged to be grossly unfair.

How often are we driven to accept an unsupported assumption because "Everybody knows that's how these things work"? It is hard to think of ourselves as second to anyone in the races we choose to enter. After all, we jump into the competition because we feel it's a job or promotion we have been working for months or years to achieve. We have honed our skills, prepared for the interview, and imagined ourselves in the position more times than we can recall. Then we don't get *the call,* we are devastated, and then we get angry. Without any effort to peer into the mirror and ask what we could have done better, we immediately embrace the notion we have suffered an injustice. When members of our family, friends, and colleagues jump on the bandwagon to support us, our embrace of a potentially incorrect conclusion only gets stronger.

All of this leaves you right where you are and represents the reason I make this point. In this moment, I am not discussing the impact of such biases on our community at large, as we must continuously work to drive prejudice, bigotry, homophobia, and a host of other afflictions out of our world. Here, I am speaking to you as an individual. If you make all the wrong assumptions, it leaves you reluctant to subject yourself to any type of critical review. This can lead to subsequent self-fulfilling prophecies because you see no need to improve any aspect of your performance. As a result, you will essentially be the same person competing for advancements, recognition, or pay increases as you were in the situation resulting in your initial failure to achieve a desi objective.

Maybe you were the most qualified and prepared, but what's the downside to temporarily putting aside hard feelings and asking yourself whether you have pursued all avenues possible to ensure that you are more than adequately prepared for the next opportunity? Perhaps your response will be a firm, "Yes, I was ready, and I am as competitive, or more so, than the selected applicant." That's fine if your conclusion is fact-based and not emotionally driven.

Don't be blinded by assumptions that only support your feelings but have little foundation in fact.

Either way, all you can do is find a way to make yourself even more competitive for the next opportunity. Perhaps much more importantly, you can also use the present situation to help shape how you will make hiring and promotion decisions if your professional journey takes you to a position where you are empowered to make such decisions.

I want to focus for a moment on the last line of the preceding paragraph. I have heard far too many of my colleagues complain about the rough road they had on their journey to their current position. I have also too often heard colleagues protest the very idea of spending a lot of time working with subordinate employees to best prepare them for advancement because nobody helped them on their way up the ladder. I am always somewhat astounded by such declarations as they ensure that nothing changes for the next generation.

We all owe to those who follow us to serve as a source of guidance and encouragement whenever such opportunities present themselves. The same struggles, obstacles, and landmines that challenge their journeys were once our own.

Any negative experience is only a *failed* experience if one takes nothing away from it. This is why I encourage anyone I mentor to focus on self-improvement, as there will never be any downside to you being the absolute best you can be. Will your journey be stalled or otherwise negatively impacted by racism, unconscious or conscious bias, or a host of other potential impacts? Absolutely possible. Once again, I feel the need to stress that I understand the world can be an awfully unfair place, and there is much work to be completed to address problems that continue to plague our society.

Again, this book is intended to help you focus on YOU. How do you navigate the white-water rapids that will undoubtedly confront you, right now, today? Racism, sexism, homophobia, etc., can be and often are real influences that can negatively affect our professional trajectories, but what we cannot do is fold up our tents and simply cave in to those factors. Let's play a vital role in setting a new dynamic in the workplace and one that requires our engagement right now.

Chapter Seven

Speaking to Power

"Sir, I owe you an apology. I was smoking pot at Lake Pulgas… I am sorry I let you defend me in front of the battalion commander, our company CO and XO, but I did smoke pot that day…

-Corporal Zedayas

Disclaimer: the situations described in this chapter are real and shared precisely as they occurred; the names used in this chapter are all fictious to avoid unnecessarily embarrassing anyone.

An assumption that one might make upon reading this book is that it is easy for me to offer the advice contained in this chapter because I am older, semi-retired and have held very senior positions in the federal government and in the private-sector. Such an assumption would be correct if I only began speaking to power when doing so no longer represented a potential stumbling block in my career. However, I have been ensuring my voice would be heard for as long as I can remember, not simply to hear the sound of my voice, but rather because a situation existed which required my engagement. I did not begin speaking to power only after achieving senior positions or having retired, both of which arguably offered me safe harbors from the potential impact speaking up could have had on my career.

I began speaking to power whenever I saw the need to do so, while everyone else chose to remain silent. I would never have suggested that becoming a career gladiator is easy or without potential consequences, and I am making no such claim here. It has always struck me as somewhat ironic that in both the public and private sectors, the conventional wisdom to ensure one has a *safe career* is to endeavor to take a path that did not make too many ripples in the pond. I can say without a shadow of a doubt I have challenged this conventional wisdom throughout my career and have never regretted doing so.

This chapter is intended to debunk the assumption that one can only speak to power once one has arrived in a position of like power.
Spectator or gladiator? You decide.

Shortly after I graduated from the U.S. Marine Corps Basic School (a kind of finishing school for newly minted Marine Corps second lieutenants), I arrived at my first duty station: 3rd Assault Amphibian Battalion, 1st Marine Division, located at Camp Pendleton, California. I was assigned to Charlie Company, and soon thereafter, assigned to lead a platoon of approximately 40 Marines. There were four black officers in a battalion that included 35-40 officers. I and another second lieutenant were brand new to the outfit, another was a mustang captain (an officer with prior time served in the enlisted ranks), and the last one was a major.

The major was bounced out of the Corps for inappropriate conduct soon after I reported to the unit, which left a total of three black officers in the battalion. One day, approximately four months into my tour of duty, half of my platoon was sent to the rifle range for rifle qualification and the other half stayed on the ramp to perform routine maintenance on the amphibious vehicles which made up the bulk of equipment for which I was responsible.

Tragically, on the range that day, a young Marine from Charlie Company put the barrel of his M-16 in his mouth and pulled the trigger. He killed himself instantly.

The firing line was immediately dismissed for the day. Three Marines, one of whom was a member of my platoon, decided to drive to Lake Pulgas, a small lake located in a very quiet and secluded part of the base. During their time at the lake, they were approached by a military police officer (MP) who apparently smelled marijuana coming from the direction of where these Marines were seated by the lake. This was 1980, and any amount of marijuana possession or usage was illegal and absolutely forbidden in the Marine Corps. The three Marines were questioned by the MP, who later charged each with smoking marijuana. The charge was based on the MP smelling what he alleged was burning marijuana as he approached the aforementioned three Marines.

No evidence was seized at the scene nor were they subjected to a blood or urine test to determine whether they had been smoking marijuana.

Eventually the Marine assigned to my platoon was brought up on charges related to his alleged marijuana smoking and was to be seen by the battalion's commanding officer for a summary court martial. A summary court martial is the lowest form of court martial, in which a single officer serves as judge and jury, and typically results in minimal forms of punishment for those found guilty as charged. Only charges analogous to civilian misdemeanors can be tried in a summary court martial. Nevertheless, a court martial of any type is a serious matter and not something any Marine wants on his or her record. A court martial on one's record will likely signal the end of their upward ascension and eventually the end of their career. As part of the proceeding, I along with my company commander and executive officer (the second in charge of a company) were eventually summoned to the office of the battalion's commanding officer (CO) to conduct the summary court martial of Corporal Zedayas.

When I reported to the CO's office, Corporal Zedayas was already present. Shortly after I arrived, the CO of Charlie Company and his executive officer (XO) arrived (the XO is the second in command in any size unit.) Once all of us were present, the proceedings began. The battalion commander, Lieutenant Colonel Pickney, read the charge and then spoke to my company commander, Captain John Malone. Lieutenant Colonel Pickney asked Captain Malone for his thoughts on the matter before us. Captain Malone said, "Colonel, I believe the MP. The Marines he caught had no reason to be at Lake Pulgas at that time and were likely there to be able to smoke pot out of view of anyone else.

MPs are taught what burning marijuana smells like and the MP has no reason to lie about the Marines involved in this matter."

Captain Malone was a fair and honest officer. I believe he spoke to the truth as he believed it to be.

Lieutenant Colonel Pickney then asked our executive officer, First Lieutenant Lewis, for his thoughts. Although I considered Lieutenant Lewis a friend and colleague, I also was fairly certain he was going to concur with whatever Captain Malone offered. That is exactly what he did, and in total fairness, he had little at his disposal to persuade him to do otherwise. Lieutenant Lewis essentially offered the same thoughts as Captain Malone, confirming his opinion that the Marines were all guilty of smoking pot and observing that none of the Marines involved had any business being at Lake Pulgas in the middle of the day.

Lieutenant Colonel Pickney, without looking up, then said to me, "And Lieutenant Mason, I assume you agree with your CO and your XO. His words were spoken more as a statement than a question. The colonel had likely concluded it was highly unlikely that the relatively new lieutenant standing before him would have the temerity to disagree with his CO or XO, and that the rest of the proceedings would move forward without any issues. The colonel was about to write something on the papers in front of him as I was coming to the position of attention. Once I assumed the position of attention, I said:

"Sir, with all due respect, I do not agree with the CO or the XO." Lieutenant Colonel Pickney looked a bit surprised, but then asked me for my thoughts.

I then told the commanding officer the following:

"Sir, on the day of this alleged incident, the Marines involved had been on the rifle range when a young Marine took his own life in a very traumatic manner. Corporal Zedayas told me he was not smoking pot at the time of his encounter with the MP. Corporal Zedayas is a good Marine with whom I have worked closely for the past four months. It should be noted that the MP found no evidence supporting his claim to include: roach clips, marijuana, rolling papers or any other typical paraphernalia associated with smoking pot. This charge is wholly reliant upon the MP believing he smelled marijuana. I am not suggesting the MP is lying, but perhaps mistaken about what he smelled. Finally, I believe Lake Pulgas, a calm, beautiful place here on the base, might be a place any of those who witnessed that tragic incident several weeks ago might go to collect their thoughts (the courts martial did not occur until weeks after the Marines were charged with smoking marijuana). Witnessing someone shooting themselves in the head with an M-16 is both a shocking and tragic incident, and I feel fairly certain that I, too, would have wanted some space to process what I had just witnessed. Lake Pulgas strikes me as the ideal spot to go to decompress. So, lacking any hard evidence, I believe Corporal Zedayas should be given the benefit of the doubt in this matter."

It did not matter to me that I was the junior officer in the room, nor that I was one of two of the most junior officers in the battalion. It did not matter to me that I was one of only three Black officers in the battalion.

It further did not matter to me that everyone in that room besides me was white, nor that all, ironically including Zedayas, were older than me. All that mattered was that I was an Officer of Marines, and in that capacity, I had very definitive leadership responsibilities. I would not have been able to sleep if I had simply gone with the flow of the proceedings and not defended my Marine for fear that doing so might adversely affect my fledgling career. It's important to note that I actually *believed* Zedayas was innocent of the charge of smoking marijuana and I was not just blindly defending one of my Marines. The point is that I had a choice to make. Period. I could have remained silent for fear of upsetting my CO or for a host of other reasons. I could have stood by as a spectator and let events unfold without my intervention.

The story doesn't end there. Lieutenant Colonel Pickney put the papers in front of him in his desk and told the assembled

Marines that he was going to hold this matter in abeyance and give it more consideration over the next day or so. I felt as though I'd achieved at least a partial victory delaying a summary judgement just for the convenience of all gathered. I thought the longer the boss thought about this matter, the greater the possibility of a finding in favor of Corporal Zedayas.

Later that same week, my platoon was scheduled to participate in sea trials with a few navy ships. As we were preparing to join the ships for this exercise, Corporal Zedayas was suddenly asked to remain in the area. By *suddenly,* I mean he had to take his gear off his vehicle and take it back to the barracks. I never suspected what was to follow, but in retrospect believe he was called back at the last minute to preclude me from joining Corporal Zedayas at what was to follow. A day or two later, Zedayas was called to the battalion front office, where he was greeted by a member of the Naval Investigative Service (now the Naval Criminal Investigative Service) who was prepared to polygraph Corporal Zedayas regarding the marijuana charge.

Rather than face the humiliation of a failed polygraph, Corporal Zedayas admitted that he and the other Marines had been smoking marijuana immediately prior to being confronted by the MP.

When I returned to the battalion area two weeks later, I was met by Corporal Zedayas. As he approached, I noted that he looked as though he'd lost 20 lbs. He was already very thin, but now looked as though he could be snatched out of his uniform without loosening any of its buttons. He did not appear to be coming with happy news, though I had no idea what he wanted to tell me. The rest of my platoon was busy taking care of a hundred tasks required for our vehicles after time spent in the salty ocean environment. The area was a hub of activity and everyone appeared excited about being home after two weeks at sea.

It was also payday, and we were due to get the next four days off (a "96" in Marine parlance), which meant there existed the combination of money and extended time off. For many of my Marines, there was nothing quite like extra liberty and a pocket full of money. Corporal Zedayas was well liked and well respected by all the members of the platoon, and some wondered aloud why he was not with us on this most recent exercise, slapping him on the back while slinging harmless jabs at him. Corporal Zedayas waded through the cacophony of noise and excitement with a heavy weight on his shoulders. I gave him a hearty "Hey, Corporal Zedayas!"

He looked very serious and my warm greeting did nothing to relax so much as a single muscle in his face. He immediately saluted me, and I returned his salute. He then got right to the point and said:

"Sir, I owe you an apology. I was smoking pot at Lake Pulgas. We quickly extinguished our joints and tossed away any evidence we had on us before the MP could clearly see us. When the MP approached us and asked whether we'd been smoking pot, we all denied it. I am sorry I let you defend me in front of the battalion commander, our company CO and XO, but I did smoke pot that day. Again Sir, I am really sorry."

Corporal Zedayas looked like hell at that moment. His eyes were swollen and bloodshot, and I could tell he had been crying immediately prior to meeting with me. He looked completely defeated. The contrast between Zedayas and every other Marine in the immediate area could not have been more striking. Whatever he was feeling in that moment had to have been magnified by all the otherwise good cheer surrounding him. I have no doubt he had punished himself far more than I could ever punish him.

He had allowed his platoon commander, just emerging from officer training and relatively new to the battalion, to begin his career as a Marine officer standing in front of senior officers and defend him when he knew all the time he was guilty. I told Corporal Zedayas that I respected the fact I did not have to learn of this outcome from someone else and appreciated the fact that he came and faced me like a man. I told him I was sorry it had come to this conclusion. I then told him I still considered him to be a good Marine and now it was time to move forward.

I never raised my voice, never swore, never made any attempt to belittle him. He knew what he had done and now, perhaps two weeks later than I would have preferred, he owned it.

The battalion commander called me to his office the next morning. He told me, "Lieutenant Mason, I am proud of you. You stood in the breach and defended your Marine based on the information you had available to you at that time. You did what a good Marine officer is expected to do. He then dismissed me, and I returned to work. Every time I recall that short conversation, I smile. The fact that my faith in Zedayas was proven to be ill-placed, there was no "I told you so" coming from anyone.

I was never really angry at Zedayas, nor did I feel any other particularly strong emotion. I did what I thought was the right thing to do. It was one of life's lessons, and in subsequent incidents involving a Marine under my charge (or other employees in my various professional roles), I did learn to ask far more questions prior to staking out a position. Zedayas was not the last Marine I defended, nor the last time I had to speak to power in my early days in the Marine Corps.

There is a second story from a bit further into my tour of duty with the Marines that bears telling here because this story involves an officer for whom I worked and who was responsible for writing my fitness report. The fitness report can make or break a career. It is an evaluation of an officer's performance and a document into which much faith is placed when considering officers for promotion. Major Hunt, my reporting senior officer at this time, was an alcoholic, and everyone in the battalion knew it, to include our commanding officer (an important point later). I was dispatched with Major Hunt to the Marine Corps base located in Twentynine Palms, California for a combined arms exercise.

During one particular phase of the exercise, in which I was not a participant, Major Hunt arrived with an element of our armored tracked vehicles. As the story was related to me by one of my sergeants, Major Hunt was riding on the very front and atop of the vehicle rather than secured in one of two hatches reserved for functions other than driving. As the vehicle came to a rest in the immediate vicinity of the infantry troops we were supporting, Major Hunt nearly fell off the vehicle.

It was clear to all in the immediate area that Major Hunt was highly intoxicated. As he stumbled and attempted to gain solid footing, a flask fell from his pocket which he was apparently too intoxicated to notice.

The flask was recovered by the same sergeant who reported the matter to me, and the incident was also witnessed by two corporals who were working with the sergeant that day. Needless to say, they were all embarrassed by this incident. We took a great deal of pride in being the best support element we could possibly be and worked very hard to support our fellow infantry Marines, some of whom already assumed anyone assigned to a mechanized unit was already a *slacker,* mostly in good humor, but nevertheless something that still bothered some of my Marines. To have the senior representative of our battalion stumbling in front of the very troops we were in the desert to support was completely unacceptable.

I was not at the location at which this incident occurred, but it was reported to me within an hour by the sergeant who recovered the flask. He was accompanied by the two corporals who witnessed the incident as well. When the sergeant moved to hand me the flask, I asked where he got it and he told me it had fallen from Major Hunt's jacket pocket. He added that this occurred right in front of the infantry unit's commanding officer. The sergeant then handed the flask over to me and asked me one simple question. He inquired, "Well sir, what are you going to do?" That was more than just a simple question. All three of the non-commissioned officers (NCOs) standing before me knew exactly what would have happened had a flask fallen out of one of their pockets and been turned over to me.

This was a question of duty and accountability. I responded, "Gentlemen, I am taking this matter to Lieutenant Colonel

Pickney." At that precise moment, I am not sure they believed anything else would happen as a result of this incident.

When we returned to Camp Pendleton, I went directly to the battalion commander's office. I was angry from the time I initially heard the story and received the flask. I was not angry because of what I knew I had to do, but rather because Major Hunt had a problem that should have been dealt with far sooner than the time of this incident and it should not have taken a report from a junior officer to drive the matter to its final resolution. He had already been to alcohol rehabilitation twice, and the second time usually results in one's discharge from the Corps. Major Hunt had evaded discharge after his second trip through rehabilitation, but sadly had not managed to escape the imprisonment of alcoholism. Unfortunately, his affliction was never adequately addressed, and instead, everyone had pretty much looked the other way.

Major Hunt arrived at more than one morning meeting already intoxicated. At one such meeting, I was trying to determine if a cigarette lighter I had found on my way to the meeting was in working condition and kept absentmindedly flicking the starter switch to see if I could get a flame. I was sitting across from a captain who noted what I was doing. He said to me, "Mason, you better not be flicking that lighter when Major Hunt gets to this table or you will blow up the whole damn room!" Several other officers seated nearby laughed heartily at the captain's remarks. So yes, everyone knew Major Hunt had a serious alcohol problem.

When I arrived at the battalion commander's office, I told him I needed to inform him of an episode of misconduct perpetrated by Major Hunt. The colonel asked me to close his door. Oddly enough, despite the fact that Major Hunt was the officer to whom I directly reported to, I was not nervous at the time I made my report. I was sharing the facts of a bad situation, not of my making, with the battalion commander. I was doing precisely what I was responsible for doing and, believe it or not, never once did I consider the possible consequences that might have resulted from my reporting a senior officer.

At the risk of sounding corny, it was simply the right thing to do. I was 24-years-old and again, one of three black officers and a very junior officer in the battalion at the time of this incident.

I had no idea of the relationship that existed between Major Hunt and Lieutenant Colonel Pickney. I did not know whether they were best friends, had served together previously or knew each other's families and shared happy times together. I knew nothing and none of that mattered.

I knew what I had to do. No options. No safe harbors. No soft shoulders to lean on. Fully in the arena. Gladiator.

The very next morning, I received a call from Major Hunt. As long as I live, I will never forget that conversation. Major Hunt said the following to me:

"Lieutenant Mason, I have a few things to say to you, and I don't need you to say anything in response. I was reported to Lieutenant Colonel Pickney for being intoxicated in the field. He had my flask in his possession. Of all the lieutenants out in the field at the time, I know that you are the only one with the intestinal fortitude to have turned me in. My Marine Corps career will be ending when I am released from the Naval Hospital. It's not the way I'd planned to leave after 15+ years of service, but that is my fault. It is likely you saved my life and my marriage and I want to thank you for that. You are a good officer and I hope you have a long and successful career in the Marine Corps."

I responded, "Major Hunt, I wish you the very best in all the challenges that lie ahead for you and your family." That was the entire conversation. I never saw Major Hunt again.

I have always appreciated the fact that Major Hunt never asked me whether his assumption was correct. He never blamed me for his problem nor did he try to escape accountability. The ultimate result of his transgression was not a small thing. Major Hunt was not being reassigned to another unit or transferred overseas or to an undesirable location to continue his career. His career was coming to an unanticipated end. There would be no celebratory retirement when he reached 20 or more years of service. There would be no lifetime health insurance for him or his family, nor any retirement income guaranteed for the rest of his life. Although one could easily argue Major Hunt's career was headed straight for a dead end for many years, and he had actually been lucky to enjoy a relatively long career.

To this day, I continue to hope he found sobriety and that the rest of his life has proceeded better than his last days as a Marine Corps officer.

I want to also share with you two important stories from my days in the FBI, which reflect the need and the manner in which one can speak to power even as a relatively junior member of an organization. The first story occurred I was a young supervisor at FBI Headquarters assigned to the Personnel Unit, Administrative Services Division. Our unit had a vacant position, and I was responsible for ranking all the applicants who had applied for the position and for ultimately creating the "package" to be sent to the Career Board to select a candidate fill the job. In FBI parlance at the time, one was considered a competitive candidate if they were in the "package" for the job, i.e., they were one of the top three candidates for the position.

Candidates ranked outside of the top three were unlikely to receive serious consideration for the posted position. I spent a considerable amount of time carefully reviewing all the resumes we received from Special Agents seeking this position. Ultimately, I ranked all of the applicants and sent that ranking to my boss, who was the chief of the unit. The list was then passed to the Section Chief, the individual to whom my boss reported directly.

Unbeknownst to me, the first time I sent the list forward, our Section Chief had a candidate he wanted selected for the position. I had ranked his preferred choice as number six, not part of the package, and therefore unlikely to be considered by the Career Board to be held to fill the position. He sent the package back to me and asked me to consider additional qualifications, each possessed by the agent he wanted selected for the position, but none having any real relevance to the job.

I sent the package back through the chain with the Section Chief's preferred candidate now ranked number five, which still put him out of the running for the position. The package was returned a second time, and this time the writing on the accompanying note was clearly written in anger as it was practically scrawled. The Section Chief was much more forceful this time and made it pretty clear who he wanted ranked within the top three.

It was at that time that I was told by my boss that the Section Chief wanted an agent who had previously worked for him and who had been of significant assistance to him during their time together.

I again considered all the candidates for the position and sent the package back up to the front office with the very same rankings I had previously submitted. My boss asked me if I was sure I wanted to do what I was doing, and I affirmed my desire to submit the list as I had created it. My boss, at that moment, earned my undying respect. It would have been easy for him to tell his hard-charging supervisor to not rock the boat and just rank the Section Chief's choice number three. He didn't, he listened to me.

I told him that this is how career selections are corrupted. Big bosses have a fair-haired guy or lady they want promoted, but don't want their fingerprints on the process. They get what they want and can lay claim to having never touched the process. If we don't stand in the breach and fight against this process, who will?

I was unwilling to be anyone's stooge and present a package not of my making, but with only my fingerprints on it. Why, you might ask, was I so willing to confront power and not yield to the desires of the Section Chief? The Section Chief wanted his "guy" to get the job, but still have plausible deniability that he had anything to do with the selection. That was unacceptable to me, and as long as I retained the responsibility for creating the career

94

board package, I had some ability and *responsibility* to impact the process.

It was a classic example of the good old boy network in operation, and I found that to be completely unfair to the other more qualified applicants within the pool.

I knew that the Section Chief had the authority to rank the candidates for the position however he chose to do so, and if that's what he wanted to do, he was going to have to do it in the open.

Well, the final note came back and ranked the candidates for the position, and to no one's surprise, the Section Chief's preferred choice was ranked #1. However, it did not escape the Career Board that the #1 candidate was clearly not the most qualified and, as a result, the second candidate — my original first choice —was selected for the position. The right decision was ultimately reached, but I am not so naïve as to believe that is always, or even most frequently, the way these stories end. Understand, I was not in a position to change the process, but I was absolutely in a position to determine how I was going to impact the process and did not shrink from that opportunity.

Although I am proud I stood in the breach and pushed back against what I saw as an unfair process, credit for this story goes equally to the man who was my boss at the time, Jimmy Carter, yes, his real name and, no, not *that* Jimmy Carter. Jimmy was willing to accept my work and stand in the breach, ready to take whatever came his way.

Jimmy took another courageous stance with the same Section Chief later that year. I was rated by Jimmy as "Exceptional" in my first year as an FBI Headquarters supervisor. The Section Chief involved in the aforementioned story told Jimmy he did not believe in rating first year supervisors as "Exceptional." Jimmy, knowing the Section Chief couldn't change the rating without a lot of heavy lifting, stayed the course and did not change my rating. Unfortunately, as it often is with small-minded people, revenge is never far off their radar. Jimmy's own evaluation suffered the consequences.

Jimmy, who had been rated "Exceptional" the year before, was downgraded at the end of the rating period. He was rated *Superior,* which was a solid rating, but second to *Exceptional* and something that mattered way too much in the FBI. Although this could have happened to anyone for a variety of righteous reasons, I will always believe he received that rating out of simple spite. Jimmy's courage in this story is something too seldomly seen in our rank-conscious, get-ahead-at-all-costs society. Jimmy was a role model to me regarding servant leadership.

I am proud of the fact that I have stood before men and women senior to me and never shied away from speaking the truth.

Could there have been consequences for the times I have spoken to and challenged conventional wisdom? Yes, there obviously could have been consequences. I feel lucky to have had very good bosses throughout my professional life who have supported me every step of the way, even when doing so put their own careers on a slightly more perilous path. However, I firmly believe that I never want to inhabit a world in which the most effective way to get ahead is by not doing the job you are paid to do, or far more importantly, the job you have taken an oath to do.

The final story I want to share with you comes again from my days as a young supervisor at FBI Headquarters. Two employees, one very junior and one relatively senior (in terms of tenure, not rank), in my unit had been caught misappropriating funds from the FBI. Misappropriation of funds is typically an offense for which termination is the best one can hope for, as a criminal prosecution is at times also a potential outcome. Though what these two employees did was wrong, I argued a different point of view when the time came to determine their fate. At the time of this incident, units could request up to $200 from the petty cash fund to buy miscellaneous supplies.

You were required to make whatever purchases were needed by your unit and return the receipts and any money not used. After making the necessary purchases receipts and any unused money, had to add up to $200. These two employees, the younger (18) of whom was a brand-new employee being led by the older employee, began using the petty cash fund as an advance on their paychecks. Their little enterprise was uncovered because they repeatedly took $200 from petty cash and a week later returned $200. The folks responsible for the petty cash fund started to think these two employees either had the worst supply inventory system ever or something was amiss. Sadly, it was the latter.

I entered the picture as a newly promoted supervisor, having arrived eight months after this matter had been initially been uncovered. I was responsible for the younger of the two employees. It took almost eight additional months before the unit responsible for adjudicating such cases was ready to deliver the verdict. I was told that the verdict was going to result in the termination of both employees. I immediately went to my Unit Chief, Jimmy Carter (the same guy who starred in the previous story) and asked for an audience with our Assistant Director (AD) to discuss the potential of a different outcome. Carter, already aware that termination was going to be the recommended outcome, nevertheless sought and received an audience with our Assistant Director.

What makes this simple fact far more noteworthy is that Carter also thought termination was the appropriate outcome. I was granted an audience with the AD a short time later. There were five people in the room, one Assistant Director, one Deputy Assistant Director, two Unit Chiefs, and one supervisor—me.

I was the junior agent and the least tenured FBI employee in the room. The AD first addressed the other three gentlemen in the room, including my boss, all concurred with the recommended punishment: termination.

When I was asked for my input, I argued three primary points:

1. The employees clearly never intended to "steal" funds from the FBI, as they returned the total amount obtained on each occasion.

2. The employees lacked a certain amount of sophistication leading them to believe as long as they replenished the funds they were provided, no harm had occurred.

3. The employees had continued to work in trusted positions for nearly a year, which I argued was an excessive amount of time to adjudicate such a simple case and that each of the employees were demonstrating their loyalty to the FBI and their hopes for some measure of mercy by their continued level of high-quality work.

The AD decided to consider the positions of all who spoke and advised he would provide us with his decision later in the day. The AD handed down his judgments later that same day. The employee who was essentially the ring leader received a 45-day unpaid suspension, and after serving her suspension and returning to work, eventually took another position elsewhere and left the FBI. The younger employee continued to do really great work and eventually, almost 20 years later, became a member of the Senior Executive Service (SES).

One should note that my arguments were not worthy of presentation before the Supreme Court of the United States and that doesn't matter. Although it was a very positive outcome, that also is not the point of this little story.

What mattered was that I was willing to take a position contrary to every other person in the room, all of whom were senior to me, to try and save two employees whose offense I did not believe merited termination.

Bottom line? If you lack the courage to speak to power, you should never be in charge of anyone but yourself. Period.

Chapter Eight

Subservience Disguised as Professionalism

"I didn't do anything because I didn't want to embarrass the presenter, who also happened to be my boss…"

-Disgruntled Mentee

The previous chapter addressed the subject of speaking to power. As I wrote earlier, I have been a mentor across the majority of professional life. Many of my discussions have involved the challenges my mentees have felt at being recognized for high quality work, assigned choice assignments and in being promoted in a fair, transparent and timely manner. I have been asked many times about the secret sauce for success. Unfortunately, there is no *secret sauce* for success in this world. However, I prefer another, more positive response to this question. I opine that success is like a good stew. It has many ingredients that must be blended properly to produce the desired outcome.

I am often asked about how to deal with situations that require tough, unpopular decisions or taking a position that runs contrary to conventional wisdom.

Ironically, many of the people I counsel are less concerned about the decision in front of them than the potential consequences the decision might have on their career. So, they remain silent or allow the moment to pass unchallenged. Examples of this include:

1. Being in a meeting in which very relevant information is conveyed incorrectly, but doing nothing to correct the situation.

2. Believing one has a better path to success of a particular project, but saying nothing when asked for input, only to see their idea presented by someone else and being widely accepted.

3. Having his or her team blamed for serious delays in the completion of a project and knowing categorically that their team completed all portions of their work on time.

4. Having desires for more complex work, potentially leading to a promotion, but being rebuffed because of the position they currently occupy, i.e., being assessed based on what they do and not who they are. Good example? A secretary who holds a relevant master's degree required for a desired position, but cannot get people to see past their current position.

This is hardly an exhaustive list. However, I want to share a story that makes the point of this chapter crystal clear. There will be times when you are going to have to choose your poison. You will be pressed in the moment to respond in a less than ideal situation.

We have to stop believing that risk is not an element of seeking a fair and transparent workplace.

I did not decide to write this book to assure you that actions we must sometimes take can always or even generally be taken without risks. I have already shared stories, each of which could have had negative consequences for me, in which I was not deterred by the potential risk to my career. I am sharing many of my own personal stories to clearly demonstrate the real stories and very real incidents which challenged me and could have negatively impacted my career. I wish I could offer a fool-proof remedy to ensure that any decision one may have to make can be made free of any consequential risks, but that is simply not possible.

I once had a mentee who sought my advice and shared the following story: He was in a meeting with many senior executives called to discuss a major project. During the meeting, information regarding the timeline his team was to meet on the project was being conveyed by his boss but was completely inaccurate. Prior to the meeting, he had shared the projected completion dates his team would meet in completing their assigned pieces of the project. He felt as a result of this inaccurate information, his team was not going to be able to meet project completion expectations and as a result, he would be blamed for the failure of the project to be completed on time.

I asked my mentee, "What was your response?" He said, "I didn't do anything because I didn't want to embarrass the presenter, who also happened to be my boss. I thought doing so would look unprofessional and I did not want such a look to be associated with me." While his desire not to embarrass his boss was a noble objective, I asked him who would defend him when his team failed to deliver their portion of the project as promised. His sullen response was predictable, "No one." I challenged his position of not wanting to embarrass his boss, first by suggesting his real motivation was more about protecting himself in the moment and not getting on the wrong side of his boss and less about not wanting to embarrass his boss. He agreed with my assessment, but continued to push back on his accountability for needing to correct the information being presented.

Remember, it's important to be honest and transparent with ourselves as well.

I asked whether he was equally concerned about all eyes turning upon him in the moment and whether he thought his facts would have supported his position. He said he was absolutely positive about his facts, but confessed to be intimidated by the senior executives in the room and decided to remain silent. He then went on to tell me that the inevitable occurred and his team was blamed for the delay in the project. Then I asked if saving his boss from the embarrassment of the moment was worth it if the cost of his silence was the appearance of his team's failure. His actual response? He stated, "Mike, I didn't deserve the criticism that accompanied my team's failure to meet unrealistic timelines. I knew the presenter was wrong and that my facts were correct!" To which I responded, "So what!" He looked at me a bit perplexed. I had no intention of leaving my "So what!" hanging in the air without an explanation. I told him everyone left that meeting with expectations built upon an error-filled presentation. Stating after the fact that you "knew…" is pointless. First, even on the remote chance someone believes you (after the fact), you now look like you had the information to correct the course of a major project and you failed to deliver.

Everything he offered in the aftermath of this situation would have just appeared to be an excuse for his team's failure.

He was adamant that his team did not fail on this project. I told him that he was absolutely right, his team didn't fail. *He* did.

My mentee was simply left to choose his poison, and he chose unwisely. There are a variety of ways he could have corrected the relevant numbers being discussed during the presentation without embarrassing his boss. Additionally, his primary objective should have been to protect his team and *himself* from the consequences of sharing inaccurate information. He should have acted in the moment to avoid finding himself sulking after a conclusion he knew was inevitable actually landed on his doorstep. You can't have it both ways.

We really need to examine the inhibitors in play when we have failed to act appropriately. It is too easy to hold others or circumstances beyond our control accountable for our failures.

Are we being silent because we are worried about peer pressure? Are we afraid to speak to our boss? Are we sure our facts are correct? Whatever the inhibitor, deal with it. I would rather my career suffer a minor setback because I stood in the breach and did the right thing than for it to suffer because I did nothing. We can all hold tough conversations around the counter sharing coffee or after work having drinks, but what about when such conversations really matter?

When I think of the sacrifices made by many others that allowed me to ascend to the positions I have held, I consider speaking up at a meeting to correct misinformation which is going to impact *my team* as a relatively minor act. If we live constantly afraid of consequences, we will never act as long as we believe the consequences of acting are more severe than the consequences of quiet acquiescence. However, when a duty to speak up is part of the equation to correct misinformation, the potential consequences of doing so must necessarily matter less.

What are some real-life tips to developing the skill and courage to speak up when required to do so? Let me offer a few, but remember, nothing I offer below is intended to suggest one will be relieved of possible negative consequences. I just consider that part of the game. I ride a motorcycle knowing full well my margin for error is a lot smaller on my motorcycle than in my car. That does not stop me from riding, it just makes me a smarter, more defensive rider. The reward I get is the intrinsic joy I experience each time I ride.

The tips below are all things I learned along my professional journey. I will briefly explore each one as we move along:

1. Know your facts.

2. Deliver your input unemotionally.

3. Think, before you open your mouth.

Now let's spend just a little bit of time elaborating on each of the tips above.

Know your facts:

When I was running the FBI's Washington Field Office, I had the pleasure of welcoming U.S. Attorney General Alberto Gonzales for a visit to our office. I briefed AG Gonzales prior to taking him into the room where the employees were gathered. I told him that he has likely heard about how offices managed their criminal and terrorism programs dozens of times, so I wanted to spend more time telling him about some of the creative initiatives the office was engaged in. I believed I had some very creative minds in that office and we were attacking some challenges in a unique way. AG Gonzales actually seemed pleased he wasn't going to receive the kind of presentation he so often received at FBI field offices. The tour went off without a hitch with one of the highlights being a presentation on our very focused community outreach program, especially to the Muslim community in the wake of the tragedy of the 9/11 terrorist attacks on America.

The next day an agent criticized me in an email that included his entire division. He noted in his email that he could not believe I allowed so much time to be spent on "soft" topics when the criminal and intelligence challenges were so intense. Had he sent me a private email registering his complaint, I would have invited him into my office and explained my reasoning for the type of briefing we prepared for the Attorney General. I would have informed him that I had shared my plan with my leadership team and all agreed that our work in "soft" areas merited the attention of the AG. However, that is not what he did. He chose to blast the boss in front of all of his colleagues. So, I decided the matter needed to be addressed in person, lest others feeling the same way might not understand how much I valued their work.

As a result, I invited his entire division, the same employees with whom he'd shared his displeasure, to a meeting the next day in one of our large meeting rooms. I identified the employee responsible for my calling the meeting, though that was not necessary because he had already done so with his email. I then went onto explain why we'd given the briefing we gave to the Attorney General.

I was not angry per se, but neither was I going to be cowed by someone whose basis for his publicly announced complaint was categorically incorrect.

I concluded my conversation with the group by inviting anyone with criticism for something we were doing in the office to bring it to my attention, and I meant it. However, I also admonished the audience to do so privately, and if they chose to "go public," at a minimum they must have their facts correct. Just for the sake of clarity, I took no further action against the employee because that was neither necessary nor appropriate. His was an error of perhaps maturity, but not, in my opinion, pursued malicious intent. I have previously invited employees to bring their complaints directly to me. He did so, if not a bit obliquely, by including me in his email distribution list.

Deliver your input unemotionally:

When I was a supervisor, I had a colleague whose every objection to everything was a combative, high strung declaration of war. Of course, I am exaggerating, but only a little bit. This individual seemingly could never disagree with someone without getting emotionally charged. No problem, challenge, objection, or observation could be made without fighting words. I consider fighting words to be the kind of words lobbed over the table that carry a message beyond the message of the words themselves. For example, words such as, "You'd have to be an idiot to believe that would work." Such words have a chilling effect on any real discussion about the subject matter at hand, at least among peers and certainly subordinates. Such words can be especially harmful to enlightened discussion if there are those in the meeting who actually do believe the idea on the table *will work*, but remain silent because they fear the wrath of the person declaring the idea dead-on-arrival. Another verbal grenade too often launched is, "Common sense dictates that…" the subtle message being anyone not in agreement must lack a certain amount of common sense. Probably the most common set of words intended to deliver a not-so-subtle message are, "As anyone with half a brain can see…"

I very intentionally avoid such language because it tends to back people into a corner and choke off other thoughtful comments on the subject.

105

Think, before you open your mouth:

In case any reader is wondering, this is the sin I have been guilty of more than any other, especially early in my professional life. It happens when I hear something I deem ridiculous and then become fixated on putting my objections on the table. That alone would not be so bad if I continued to actively listen to the presenter, which, early in my professional career, I often did not do. I was often guilty of "small ball" thinking, i.e., thinking of only immediate impact of the idea would have on my group. That would also be okay if my group constituted more than a small percentage of the overall population impacted by the discussion. A simple and quick example? I was in a meeting once during which there was a clear need for employees to act a bit more aggressively in certain situations, such as when interviewing a subject and being easily defeated by behavior polite society is unaccustomed to addressing.

At one point in the meeting, I blurted out "I want stallions working for me!" I probably said it several more times during the same meeting.

Well, I later changed that line to "I want thoroughbreds working for me." The latter phrase is devoid of gender. You might have smiled at the former phrase unless you were a woman and thought the use of "stallion" was intentional.

I have learned to govern my mouth when the urge to speak up is driven by an emotional button being pushed.

All that means is that I first think about my audience and what it is I am trying to achieve. I now seriously consider whether I need to say anything at all. The important thing is to get comfortable speaking up in meetings, town halls, all-hands and any other gathering where your input has been solicited. Speak up when necessary to challenge conventional wisdom or to offer a different point of view. I have sought follow-on conversations with many subordinates during which I targeted them for future promotions and/or special assignments because I liked the way they handled themselves under pressure. I once had a young employee, Jackie, who was scheduled to make an important presentation to her team. Little did she know the meeting would be attended by the director in charge of her team (and her manager's boss); her father, who also worked in our organization; and by me, the head of the department.

She was clearly nervous throughout most of her presentation, but she was a gladiator. First, she was incredibly well prepared. It appeared she had considered every possible question we could ask as she batted answers back like a well-conditioned tennis player slaps forehands over the net. Next, she knew exactly the message she wanted to deliver and then ensured she stayed on track to deliver that message. Finally, and most impressively, she even anticipated what needed to be true with every contributor to her plan for it to work and was not the least bit shy about making those points crystal clear. This was going to be team effort, but she left no doubt as to who would be responsible for managing that effort.

I was thoroughly impressed with her presentation. She was not only a very young employee (~24), but she was also new to the company having been employed for less than a couple of months. Nevertheless, her presentation was far superior to those I'd seen from some senior managers in our department.

Remember that your message will be carried by its logic and the manner in which you present it. While you may be given a bit of grace because of your youth and relative short tenure in the position or because of your lack of experience making presentations, why not seize the opportunity to make a positive impression? No one goes into a meeting in which they are to make a presentation seeking to fail. However, far too many go into such meetings just hoping to survive. Gladiators may stumble or get a question that temporarily knocks them back on their feet, but they overcome these setbacks and forge on because they are well prepared. Gladiators go into meetings planning to impress because they are READY to impress.

Chapter Nine

Defining Success

"Dad, I just want to earn enough money to not have to worry about money."

-Matthew Mason

At no time throughout the writing of this book have I attempted to define success, and despite those very words serving as the title of this chapter, I believe success has to be customized to fit each individual's desires. What I am going to attempt to do is offer a simplified version of two things:

1. My personal definition of success.

2. Why it is important to succinctly define success in your life.

Webster's dictionary offers several variations of the word that include:

➢ The accomplishment of an aim or purpose.
➢ A favorable outcome; positive result; triumph or victory.
➢ The attainment of wealth, fame, or social status.

I mildly believe some aspects of the aforementioned, but I more firmly believe the definition of success should continue to evolve for all of us. It is less a destination than it is a continuous journey. I don't want to reach any point in my life and declare that I am done. This is an important concept as I have encountered many young people who get frustrated early into their professional careers because they have allowed themselves to define success only by acquiring the ultimate goal they have set for themselves.

I've heard many say, "I want to own my own company" or, "I want to be a CEO." Both are lofty goals and there is absolutely no reason to avoid striving for such ambitious, but those are long-term goals. Much like the building of a cathedral, the construction of all great works must start with a foundation and then, brick by brick, a work of beauty is erected. I like to think the cathedral of my life that I am building will not be fully constructed until I have lived my final day and my ashes are spread to the winds. At that time, by definition, my personal evolution, the cathedral of my life, will be complete.

A number of former mentees that I have counseled have left me concerned because of how resigned they had become to forgoing goals they had previously set for themselves. Some limited the possibility of reaching goals even just beyond their current status. I have found that the primary cause of this loss of motivation, focus, and drive is because they set lofty goals but did not consider the intermediary steps, many of which are often difficult in themselves to achieve. They (mentees) typically failed to establish metrics of success for steps which must be achieved on the road to the accomplishment of their goals. There have been times when simply discussing where they are now and where they were five years ago lends more clarity to the progress they actually already achieved toward a goal they have set for themselves.

Imagine a 35-year-old devout couch potato, who has never run a mile, deciding she wanted to run a marathon. If her first step in achieving this lofty goal was to start by running half a marathon, she would almost certainly fail. Reaching the goal of running a marathon requires commitment, perseverance, discipline, and consistency in training just to name some of the elements of successfully achieving this goal. It also requires a commitment to succeed in small increments. No one who is not already a dedicated runner decides to run a marathon and goes out to run one two weeks later. However, if this same person (and now former couch potato) looked at her progress three months from the date she began training and realized she could now run six miles, she might be elated (glass half full) or seriously disappointed as a marathon is 26.2 miles. How short-sighted would that be? You couldn't run a hundred yards three months ago and now you are running six miles without stopping! If you have no metrics of success, how do you measure progress? So, stop thinking about your ultimate objective and start establishing more short-term goals.

I suspect that some people feel disappointment when reflecting on the relative success of their life. When I have heard friends or colleagues express such sentiments, I find myself wondering if they ever paused to actually define what success means to them. I further wonder whether they ever set interim goals or some other metric of success against which they could take stock of the current status of their life. I suspect having done so, they might have a greater appreciation of their current status and perhaps be more motivated to reach higher.

It is worthwhile to note that I do not define success in terms of material wealth, senior status, broad authority, or any other conventional description of success.

When I write that I have been concerned about a mentee's commitment to success, I am referring to success as they define success. I am not defining their failure to achieve a typical metric society might use to describe success, nor how I define success. I do not focus on anything other than their definition of success.

When my two sons —Matthew and Benjamin —were young boys, we went on a camping trip and decided to go kayaking down the James River in Virginia. Our trip required that we be driven far upstream. From there, we launched our individual kayaks and enjoyed a two-to-three-hour paddle down the river. The individual responsible for loading our kayaks and driving us to our drop-off point was one of the happiest people I have ever met. He talked about what we might see as we paddled back to the campground and then generally described his work responsibilities.

He was someone who clearly loved his job, and he was not an 18-year-old summer employee. He was in his early thirties and had been working at the campground for approximately ten years. He told us that in the winter he transitioned to other roles at area ski resorts and shared that he loved the freedom his life afforded. I was genuinely impressed by how utterly content he was with his life. You could literally feel his joy. He loved the outdoors and loved introducing newcomers to the wonders of his world.

I did not stand in judgement of this individual. However, I grew up with a father who was born in 1930 (in the wake of the Great Depression) and whose singular focus his entire adult life was reaching some level of financial security. I have already advised the reader that my father was not an overly generous man and watched his every dollar very closely. My neighbors were mostly cut from a similar mold, though they were all generous with their time with me. In my neighborhood, a "good job" was one that offered steady work of 40 hours per week, paid vacations, medical benefits, and the king of all attributes: a guaranteed retirement annuity. I would have been judged a success by most of my neighbors if I had gotten a job that offered those four attributes. To be clear, those are not bad measures of success, they are just not my definition of success or at least not the *only measures* of success that were important to me.

As my sons and I listened to our river guide, all I could think about were the following three things:

1. What's he going to do when he reaches retirement age?

2. I wonder if he has good health insurance.

3. How does he survive in a bad winter with little snow and few skiers?

In other words: yes, I am my father's child! I did want the aforementioned attributes offered by many jobs, but I wanted much more as well. Nevertheless, I never once mentioned my concerns

111

about our guide's chosen line of work. Rather, I told my sons that our river guide represented my definition of success.

At the time, I was already a senior executive with the FBI and my sons were puzzled by my enthusiastic embrace of our guide's chosen line of work. So, they asked me how I could so easily define our guide as a success story. They ultimately asked me the next logical question, "How do you define success?"

I responded that I define success, at least in part, as loving your work. It is about doing that work with passion and caring about the quality of your work every day. I looked forward to going to work just about every day of my professional life. Yes, I have had some days that were less than great, but I always awoke the next day looking forward to going to work again. Even in my earliest days of employment working very low-level jobs, I found a way to love what I was doing. If I hated my job—which I honestly never did—I would have looked for another job. While I realize many folks who hate their jobs can't simply leave on a spur-of-the-moment decision, they can engage to either find a different job in the company in which they work or look for work in another company altogether. However, it is also patently absurd to work in a job you hate for 35 years and think there is anyone to blame but yourself.

I have always brought a positive attitude to every job I have ever held. I have always been able to find something to enjoy.

Our river guide was not worried about health insurance or a pension. He was living for today. He decided to let the future take care of itself, and I admired his free spirit attitude, if not his seemingly complete disregard for "security." Hey, I am who I am!

Success is also not about how much money one makes. It is about being content with the life your income affords you. My son Matthew once told me, "Dad, I just want to earn enough money to not have to worry about money." Now some may think that is what we all want and that was an obvious statement. However, knowing my son, I knew he was saying that he wanted to earn enough

112

money to live a life not driven constantly by the need to earn more and more money. He did not want money to define his ambitions nor let his ambitions be deterred by money alone. I knew my son was going to manage his life in a manner that his income supported versus constantly looking for a *better job*, i.e., one that paid him more money to support an ever-expanding lifestyle. He was not going to find himself having *champagne taste and beer money*. I also knew—and he has since proven me correct—that he was not going to *live to work,* but rather was going to *work to live.* Think about that before moving on. Those are two distinctly different ambitions. He was going to make maximum use of his income but was never going to find himself in debt pursuing activities or material possessions far beyond the limits his income could support. Neither was he going to be defined by his income.

I strongly believe that many of the financial challenges confronting people today come from an inability to distinguish needs from wants. No one needs to own $250.00 sneakers, but how many people will put such purchases on a credit card with a minimum monthly payment plus interest. It's a sure way to financial hell, but I digress.

I must admit, I spent too much of my professional life living to work. I did not do vacations well, never went home for lunch even when I lived less than three miles from my job, was almost always the first person in the office and too often the last to leave. I rarely just took a day off… just to stop and smell the roses. I allowed and encouraged those working for me to take time off over the holidays. I too often told my wife I needed to let those who had worked so hard all year take time off during the Christmas to New Year's Day holidays. That often meant I was among the few people working over the holidays. My logic, or lack thereof, never changed across my career. I am proud that I have worked hard all my life, but I am not proud of these particular things, as I believe I paid a price for my misguided focus. As I wrote previously, I have never wanted to be the human version of a tumbleweed, blown about by the vagaries of the wind, but I could have stood down a lot more than I did.

I would rather define what success means to me and pursue that specific objective. Too often, we are more than willing to find convenient parking spaces for our ready-made excuses for discontinuing the pursuit of our professional objectives. "I can't succeed in this company with the current management" or, "My boss is a jerk, so I have no hope of getting promoted in the next few years." "I did dream of becoming a pilot, but the time to pursue that dream has passed." Maybe it is too late to pursue becoming a commercial or fighter pilot, but not too late to earn a private pilot's license.

Many other convenient excuses are just that—excuses. A mentee once said to me, "Mike, I am just not happy here doing what I am doing." My response to her was, "Well, where would you like to be and what would you like to be doing?" Her response? "I don't know, I just know I am not happy here." How do I pursue an unknown destination? I have never gotten into my car, started the engine and drove off with zero idea of where I was going. We cannot wait for our desires to take shape by fate or just settle with wherever life takes us as long as it's away from *here.*

There was a saying when I was in the Marine Corps that went as follows: "The two best duty stations in the world are the one you just left and the one you are going to next."

That statement was of course not true, but it spoke to our inability to make where we are at this moment good for us. We look back with affection upon a past job, one in which we found all manner of faults at the time we worked there. Then, we look forward with an eager anticipation to our next adventure because the pasture is always greener ahead, right?

How many people actually take the time to do more than simply show up for work? How many define what success means to them individually? I like to think of my own success as climbing the steps on a ladder. While I knew what I wanted to achieve everywhere I have worked, those achievements were steps, not final destinations. I have had a plan for myself covering the next six months of my life for as long as I can remember.

114

When I was a young officer in the Marine Corps, I would actually write out a dozen or so goals and then—I know, this is kind of anal—I graded myself on each goal at the end of the period covered by those goals (usually six months).

My goals ranged from motivating and refocusing a good Marine who had lost his way to saving a certain amount of money to reaching specific fitness benchmarks. Regardless, they always included things I needed to do to satisfy my various ambitions. I concentrated on areas in which I knew I needed a great deal of improvement. In the FBI, I initially focused on my public speaking skills. I witnessed and admired so many speakers for their calm delivery in front of audiences numbering in the hundreds. I knew I wanted to learn how to be equally comfortable and smooth speaking before large audiences. I have already shared with you in a previous chapter the intentional manner in which I went about improving my ability to speak before large audiences.

So, success, much like failure, is not a final destination. It helps enormously if you can define the former as you proceed through your professional journey. You needn't worry about the latter. Failure will come even at times when your preparation has been thorough. What does success look like for you in the next three months, six months or year? What must you do to achieve success in that specific swim lane? Who can help you? If you cannot answer these questions, perhaps this is as good a time as any to give that question a bit of considered thought. Whatever else you do, don't be resigned to working in a job for which you have no passion or one that brings you no level of personal satisfaction. Life is far too short.

Chapter Ten

Never a Tumbleweed

When I was in seventh grade and told a close relative of my desire to become an FBI Special Agent, she replied, "That is never going to happen."

-A Potential Dream-Killer

My intentional focus in this book has been on the individual...you. Just as when we are captured in a rainstorm, life _always_ gives us options. One can pop an umbrella up, put on a raincoat, run and find shelter or simply get wet. The same is true in life. Our options are not always great choices, but I can think of few situations that present themselves without alternatives. Yes, we are all going to die one day. No options there. However, this book is about living! A tumbleweed is something blown about by the vagaries of the wind, no destination, beholden only to its immediate atmosphere. I have known too many humans who metaphorically act as tumbleweeds. Folks who bounce from one job to the next. No plan, no ultimate goals, just taking whatever life dishes out.

I remember watching a game show on television and the question asked of the contestant was as follows: "On a scale of 1-10, how high does the average person rate their job?" The contestant responded, "1" and had a look on her face that suggested, "isn't that how everyone feels about their job?" Tumbleweed! She must have assumed absolutely no one loves their job, which could only be a reflection of her path to success or my conclusion that she didn't have one! If you feel you would rate your job a stinking "1," my question to you would be, "why are you still there?" I know, I know. One cannot just walk away from their source of income. I have been very fortunate to never hold a job I hated. I had a few jobs that made it clear to me what I did not want to do the rest of my life, but never a job that I hated. However, when I did indulge in employment that I didn't exactly *love*, I didn't spend my valuable time complaining; I spent time looking for a better opportunity.

I speak to people all the time who seem to believe they have somehow been imprisoned by their current job and have no options, so they stay and grouse endlessly. I firmly believe that if you show me a chronic complainer with 30 years in the same position or with the same company, that person was complaining endlessly after six months on the job. No one has ever owned my destiny, my spirit, my motivation or my ambition. If you stay engaged in the same employment for the money, at least make the job work for you. If you think your boss is an idiot, work to become a boss, just not the same type of manager or supervisor you dreaded having as your own.

This entire narrative has been my attempt to use stories to convey important points. If I could shed the world of one "feeling" or "attitude," it would be that of victimization. I am never going to be anyone's *victim*. There are over seven billion people in the world and only about a half dozen have any hope of ever hurting my feelings. I care about many people, even those I don't know, but the vast majority will never wield any power over me, nor should you allow them to do so with you. I realize that much of what I have espoused in these pages is *"easier said than done,"* but the same is true of any of the dreams we might hold close. Lacking intentional focus and effort, our dreams will remain just that…dreams, something we are *wishing* might come true. We have to turn those dreams into goals and move from *wishing* to *working*, because that is what separates dreams from goals. You might do everything right and ultimately miss reaching one or more of your goals. Nevertheless, you will be most unlikely to accomplish anything worthwhile if you do not take that first step.

The characterization of one as a *victim* indicates the fight is over, done, finished. I have been knocked on my butt many times,

117

but I have never remained down. I write this not as a point of bragging, but as a genuine point of pride.

It strikes me that we are becoming a permanent victim-state in the United States. I feel as though we have loss any sense of personal accountability and constantly look for someone or something to blame for our woes.

I know what follows is likely to be met with harsh criticism, but I am writing from my heart and will take that chance.

I was once listening to a National Public Radio (NPR) interview with a patient advocate during which she said we need to remove the stigma of drug addiction because it is a *disease*. The advocate went onto say that we have to remove the shame that is often felt by drug addicts. Let me preface what follows by saying that I have a ton of empathy for people who find themselves addicted to drugs or alcohol. I have seen the prison one inhabits when addicted to drugs or alcohol. I have witnessed firsthand the damage addiction can do, not only to one suffering from addiction, but often their extended family as well.

I fully support the development of more treatment centers at which addicts can be treated. However, I have known many alcoholics and drug addicts, and in my 63 years of life, I have not met a single one who never consumed drugs and/or alcohol. I have absolutely zero concern that my friends and colleagues, who do not drink excessively, will ever suffer the *disease* of alcoholism. They may catch the flu or suffer from a bad cold or a dozen other maladies we have all faced at one time or another, but I feel confident they will never become alcoholics.

I have never smoked pot or used any illegal drugs, and similarly have zero fear that I could one day, absent the steady ingestion of cocaine, heroin, or any other illegal narcotic, somehow become a drug addict.

I have now even heard obesity characterized as a disease. It has nothing to do with consuming too many calories or failing to exercise, it's apparently not something anyone can prevent. This is not a tirade against the obese, drug addicts, or alcoholics, but it is a tirade against the notion that we have no control over what or who we become. I love food, and I love eating, but I work each day to manage my weight. I have good and bad eating days, but I own them all. I do believe some people are more prone to various types of addictions than others and may, as a result, fall prey to addiction more readily than others. Obesity is undoubtedly impacted by environmental forces. If food was used to comfort unhappy children, those same children may be more likely to continue into adulthood seeing food as a source of comfort. However, I simply do not buy this movement toward absolving individuals of any accountability for the condition in which they find their lives. If I am not responsible for my life, who is? Who cares more about what becomes of me than me?

I feel the same way about a thousand other conditions we sometimes find consuming our lives. I may get knocked down from time to time, but I categorically refuse to be anyone's victim.

So, excuses such as, "I am terrified of speaking in front of people!" work only if that is where you plan to stay. The same goes for every other excuse that keeps one from becoming self-actualized. I'd rather hear someone say, "Oh my God, I am absolutely terrified of speaking in front of audiences, but I also know I will have to get over this fear if I intend to succeed as I have planned."

Let me be clear that the success of one's life is not, in my opinion, measured by the acquisition of material assets. I will ultimately measure the success of life by the energy I put into achieving the goals I set for myself, not just at the beginning of my adult life, but rather the goals I set for myself along the way, throughout my life's journey, to include this time of my life.

I may not achieve all of those goals, but my question to myself will be whether I apply myself completely to achieving my goals. I never want my *bucket list* to be empty. When I accomplish the next thing on that list, I want to add something else to the bottom.

Naturally, as with all of us, I have failed to satisfy some goals that were one-time opportunities. Remember me making reference to wanting to be liked and how that has worked against me at times? I have failed to call out someone for an inappropriate comment, failed to recommend the dismissal of an employee who richly deserved to be fired, and occasionally failed to chew out someone for an offense meriting a good ass chewing. In just about every instance, it was my quest to be seen only as a positive influence that kept me from acting. I have done all of the aforementioned many times in my professional life, but most of us remember with far more clarity the times we wish we had acted differently, but failed to do so. I have failed to engage in matters that required my attention because I spent far too much time considering how my engagement should manifest itself and before long, the time for engaging had passed. I have said things for which I probably should have apologized. In each such instance, I believe I have caught myself, but acknowledging an oversight to oneself is not even close to acknowledging it to the person or people impacted. I am not seeking perfection, but rather a recognition of areas of my life which needs improvement as we all should do on a routine basis.

Again, I don't want to be a tumbleweed or dismiss failures by retreating to that safe harbor of "I didn't really want that anyway." Recently, I found myself wondering how we define *old*. Most of us are willing to acknowledge when we reach *middle age*, but much less comfortable describing ourselves as old, besides doing so in a joking manner. So, this became a question I wanted to spend a bit of time defining for myself. I had a conversation with my brother and with a cousin during which I posed the question: "How do you define old?"

Ultimately, we arrived at a similar concept of old age being a time when we have ceased to evolve, ceased to learn, ceased embrace new challenges. It's that time when we essentially are all we are ever going to be. Given that conceptual idea of old age, that is a place I never plan to be! I get it: ninety-nine is old in anyone's book, but I am seeking to move beyond the number and toward a definition that has more meaning to me. This concept also allows me to resist the aforementioned factors related to old age. I will age no matter what I do, but I don't have to stop evolving or pursuing new adventures until my health, or my energy demands a quieter lifestyle.

Early in my professional life, I heard the statement, "I just don't know where all the years have gone." I vowed never to be guilty of that utterance. I was motivated to write this book because I wish for everyone to live their own lives with gusto. I think of my life as a great Thanksgiving Day dinner when the turkey was accompanied by some of that unbelievably scrumptious gravy! On such occasions, I always saved a bit of a dinner roll or biscuit to ensure I had something to sop up every bit of that good gravy. I wasn't leaving anything to be washed away. That is the model for how I have lived my life and how I intend to continue doing so. I represent the biscuit and life's adventures represent the gravy.

I also do not want this book to be one of exceptionalism, i.e., I thrived in a system which had all the ills our society is afflicted with, so why can't you?

We do not all possess the same DNA. Nevertheless, residing in a place of permanent unhappiness or where you never reach a feeling of fulfillment or — at the very least — to have never strived to reach those goals set for yourself and not goals established by others, strikes me as unacceptable. There are potholes, sharp curves, and a host of other obstacles awaiting all who strive to reach a state of self-actualization. There will be failures and unfair challenges and outcomes, but to all of that I say with all my heart and soul, so what? We cannot allow others to own our spirit, our energy, or our motivation.

Any time I have stumbled I have rarely become disheartened. Such a state of mind strikes me as an endpoint and I just never want an endpoint in my life to reflect a serious failure. I simply figured out that I needed to know with a greater degree of specificity what was required and commit myself to doing better the next time. When I have been criticized, I have looked for guidance from the person whose critique of my work has struck a chord in me.

Regarding the Academy staff member who so harshly graded my paper (as described earlier in the book), I was never given the opportunity to have a conversation with the individual responsible for grading my paper. As a result, that critique represented the vagaries of the professional winds we all face at one time or another. The comments of the grader were a strong and negative wind, but those winds did not move me off the course I had charted for myself—not even for even a second. Ultimately that is what truly matters. I could have buckled and decided I did not have the right stuff to become a Special Agent of the FBI, but I did not. I could not control what that instructor wrote nor felt about my candidacy to become an agent. All I could control was my response. That is true in most of the situations we confront throughout our lives. I was not going to be the victim of an anonymous grader.

The choice to control our response is powerful. I have spoken to many high school classes and the one piece of counsel I always offer students is the power they have to make choices in their own lives. I practically plead with them to never yield that power to anyone else.

Peer pressure is just that, pressure put on one by their peers. It is not a mandate. It is not the law. It does not eliminate one's ability to make a decision. The choice to drink alcohol prior to reaching the legal age, smoke pot, or use harder drugs, is just that, *a choice.* I remember when Nancy Reagan, the wife of then-President Ronald Reagan, started an anti-drug campaign with the simple phrase, "Just Say No!" She was attacked for creating an overly simple strategy to combat drug use. However, I thought she was absolutely spot on in her campaign. Let's not make this overly complicated: deciding to ingest drugs is a choice. I am glad I grew up with "fear pressure" because I knew my father was not going to accept drug use in our home. The fear pressure I felt, and I should say, *I embraced,* was far greater than any peer pressure I ever felt.

Nevertheless, my father was not at my side for 98% of my teenage years, and I, just like everyone else, had a choice to make when confronted with options of going along with the crowd or staking out a position of my own. When we relieve people, including young teens, of their responsibility to make appropriate decisions, we effectively give them license to fail. I have listened to far too many parents suggest that their child was always well behaved and always made good decisions until they fell in with the *wrong crowd.* So, this really bright child suddenly had no other *choice* but to join the wrong crowd and continue down the wrong path? He or she had no ability to make a choice that was best for themselves? That is absurd. I have never looked to others to guide my decisions.

I had my first alcoholic drink on my 21st birthday, and as I had planned, I shared that drink with my father. I bought a bottle of Chivas Regal and poured my father a drink and poured one for myself.

I then grabbed a can of coke, popped the lid, and moved to pour some into my glass to dilute what I was sure was going to be a distasteful drink. I was far more into the ceremony than the choice of drink. My father practically jumped out of his seat and told me: "If we are going to do this, we are going to do it right!" He told me we needed to drink it straight. So, I clinked glasses with my father and took my drink down in one swallow. If I think about it today, I can still feel the burn of that whiskey going down my throat. I subsequently wondered if my father made me drink it straight knowing how distasteful I would find it and therefore shy away from its consumption going forward.

I had dozens of opportunities to drink alcohol before I reached the State of Illinois' legal drinking age of 21, but I very consciously chose not to do so. This is not to suggest that every teenager who consumed alcohol before reaching the legal age is a bad person—hardly. The vast majority are young people just flexing their wings. I am only making a statement that one will be confronted with choices throughout one's life, and the sooner we learn to make and embrace our own choices, the better off we will be. Even if we occasionally make poor choices, we will own the consequences and steer the ship of our lives better when confronted by the next storm. We will at least own the fact that we were not taken in by others and simply following the crowd which led us to a place we would really rather have avoided.

If we constantly look to pass off our decisions on others or circumstances we don't control, we will be forever victims of something or someone.

This brings me to one final piece of advice I am going to offer to readers of this book, especially those just entering the working world. Don't be a lemming. Always remember the day you interviewed for your job or the day you decided to pursue a particular field and all you thought you would bring to your work. Let that be your guide throughout your career. Let me share a few stories from my own work history to illustrate this point with practical clarity.

As previously mentioned, I accepted a job a gas station pumping gas. I was 15-years-old and at that time no one pumped their own gas. This was a time when gas station attendants pumped your gas, cleaned your windshield, checked your oil, and a host of other automobile tasks we all do for ourselves today. However, I digress. When I was hired to pump gas, I felt as though the quality of my service brought in more customers which thereby secured my job. I treated that station as though I owned it. I swept, cleaned bathrooms, stacked oil, and did a myriad of other chores the afternoon crew, all grown men, never did.

I didn't care. I always believed that busy equaled job security. I have previously managed employees and stressed the same philosophy throughout my entire professional life.

In the summer of 1977, I remained on campus and worked painting dorm rooms. My partner and I had a system: we would go into each room, apply tape where the walls met unmovable furniture, and make other preparations in a very organized manner before we started painting. Before long we were painting five rooms a day. The vast majority of the crew would spend the morning, if not just about the entire day, sleeping. The boss of the painting crews was an older gentleman who didn't seem to care whether one room per day was painted or five. My partner and I never received any special recognition for our work; we were not paid more nor were we relying on the boss for any type of future recommendation. We worked as we did because we were being paid to work eight hours a day. It is no more complicated than that—eight hours of work for eight hours of pay. I was very happy to learn the guy I was teamed with that summer embraced the same attitude.

I have heard far too many people state that their disdain for working hard came from watching others who were being paid the same hourly wage or the same salary who didn't seem to work hard at all. They came in late, left early and applied minimum effort to their daily productivity. I have even been challenged and teased for working hard when many around me were not. When I was painting rooms, I was directly asked why I worked so hard to paint five rooms a day when just about everyone else was painting one room a day? My answer then and every subsequent time I have been asked a similar question remains the same: my contract is not with my coworkers; my contract is with the employing entity. They told me they would pay a specific wage for working eight hours a day. I am merely holding up my end of that bargain.

I firmly believe that one ingredient every secret sauce for success must contain is hard work. I do not care about any of the challenges one might be confronted with on the job, hard work is its own reward.

I have zero doubt that my work history, which includes no periods of involuntary unemployment, is directly connected to one factor: I have always worked hard. I know how simple this sounds, but in 45+ years of work, I have never personally known or seen evidence to suggest hard work represents anything other than a benefit to one's career aspirations. Am I suggesting the hardest worker will not be laid off to preserve a position for a favorite of the boss? I am not. Neither am I suggesting that hard work always leads to appropriate promotions. Hey, life ain't always fair. What I am suggesting are the vagaries of the professional winds we will all face must not define the effort, enthusiasm or passion we apply to our work. I work hard for me; my employer is just the other beneficiary of my work with me being the primary beneficiary.

There is no one on the face of earth more accountable for our success than the person we see in the mirror. It's funny how we tend to point to a half dozen external factors when we are rationalizing why we were not selected for a job or a promotion. Sometimes those external factors played a major role in one's failure to be selected or promoted. Sometimes the selecting official of a team consisting of only of men leaned away from better qualified females when backfilling a vacant position. Sometimes race, religion, sexual preference, and a host of other irrelevant factors impacted our failure to be selected.

I hope the message I have expressed throughout this book makes it clear how very aware I am of such negative impacts. My point is when we must not allow those negative impacts to determine our enthusiasm for preparing for the next opportunity or determine whether we will even pursue the next opportunity. When I was in seventh grade and told a close relative of my desire to become an FBI Special Agent, she replied, "That is never going to happen." What was the lesson I took from her negative prediction and failure to offer me any encouragement at all? I learned not to discuss my future plans with her, and I did not. Those words did not make me pause and reconsider my professional dreams, they merely eliminated one important subject she and I would never again discuss.

You do not need people pulling down your hopes and dreams like a ship's anchor. Even if she fervently believed that a Black kid being raised on the Southside of Chicago had *zero* chance of becoming an FBI Special Agent, she could have said, "Honey, I wish you the very best. I hope you achieve your dream one day."

So, my friends, the journey to success is not about the obstacles and hurdles you will face as you pursue your life's professional ambitions. Rather, it is about how you address those obstacles.

It is about the application of effort, commitment and focus on achieving YOUR professional objectives. I hope this book has given clarity to at least one concept: we are most accountable for whatever we do or accomplish in this life. We do not reside in a perfect world and cannot wait for the world to evolve to that point to begin our journey.

There will be rain, snowstorms, and maybe even a few tornadoes, but if our spirit, attitude, passion, and motivation remain strong, the odds for achieving success are in our favor. The winds of life may at times push us a bit off course, but that only signals the need to grab hold of the rudder, set our sails, and strengthen our focus. It is never the time to simply stop, recalibrate, and modify our goals to suit others. Perish the thought. Carpe Diem! However my life ends one day, I hope I will be seen as a gladiator to the very end.

Made in United States
Orlando, FL
23 June 2023

34456154R00075